Life on the Prairie

Memories of a North Dakota Boy

By Ken Stein

authorHOUSE®

AuthorHouse™
1663 Liberty Drive, Suite 200
Bloomington, IN 47403
www.authorhouse.com
Phone: 1-800-839-8640

First published by AuthorHouse   9/27/2007

ISBN: 978-1-4343-0236-6 (sc)

Library of Congress Control Number: 2007903143

Printed in the United States of America
Bloomington, Indiana

This book is printed on acid-free paper.

This project is dedicated to my best friend and brother, Rob. His love of the outdoors was an inspiration to me. This was Rob:

He always had that special knowing smile for his friends and family, he was the first one to charge into the fray, he was tireless, his shooting was deadly accurate, he loved hunting, and hunting fit him like a glove. He was a warrior. He was my brother. He was the modern outdoorsman personified. No one had the zest for the outdoor life like Rob. He took me to my limit many times and I loved him for it. And I miss him horribly. There isn't a day that goes by that I don't think of him, even though we haven't hunted, fished, camped or just hung out together for many years. He had MS, one of God's most insidious tools to test a man's faith. I know that life is fleeting and eternity is endless and therein lies my hope for him. The only thing that makes sense is this: There must be something pretty special in eternity for this warrior that was crippled at such a young age. It's the only thing that I can hang onto to quell the anger that I feel for having him taken away from us so early. I'm talking about someone special. I'm talking about Rob. He was tall, he was slim, he was strong, he loved his family, he was intelligent, he was the most courageous person I've ever known, he was a warrior. He was my brother.

Robert K. Stein born 1957-died 2005

Preface

One of the things I've often thought about over the years is what keeps us in North Dakota? If you ask that question of a hundred people you may get a hundred different answers. Although the answers seem to vary, most have a common theme. Somewhere in their answer the word 'freedom' appears. Another word that appears almost as often is 'outdoors'. So, we're going to take some looks at how our freedoms and our closeness with nature have enhanced the quality of our lives. You'll notice right away a lot of our looks are with our tongue in cheek. This lighthearted look at our lives on the plains is guaranteed to bring back a lot of memories. When I started compiling my material, I found that most of what I remembered best are the experiences that were most emotional and funny or both, which is only natural. When something special happens it finds a permanent place in most memories. As we live our lives, we discover that we all need reminders of the past and where we're from to keep things in proper perspective. In the end that's what this book is all about, staying in touch with our roots. I thought I knew a little about writing, but it quickly became obvious that this project is showing me just how little knowledge of writing I do have. It certainly became a huge learning process. So, what started out as a book of memories in a lot of ways became much more.

It became part of my own life long journey. I'm not sure if this will ever be finished, at least in my mind. There is always at least one more thing to relate. I've tried to be as honest as my memory will allow, although I'll be the first to admit that I may have embellished some things just a little. If this is interesting to you, maybe you'll capture some of what it feels like to be as free as we are and what life is like out here on the prairies of North Dakota.

Contents

CHAPTER 1

WHO ARE THESE NORTH DAKOTANS?

You're curious, I know. You're thinking, "Why haven't I heard of anyone from North Dakota?" That's probably because there just aren't very many of us up here, only around 630,000 total, or about 1/5 of the Minneapolis/St. Paul three million plus metro area population. North Dakota has 70,000+ square miles within its borders, so with only 630,000 people living here, we are spread so thin that everyone pretty much has to shout to be heard. In fact, in the lower 48, only Wyoming and Montana, with densities of 5 and 6 people per square mile respectively are less densely populated. North Dakota has about 9 people per square mile. As a comparison, on the other side of the coin is the northeastern state of Rhode Island with a population density of about 700 people per square mile. That means there are nearly 80 times more people per square mile in Rhode Island than in North Dakota. It would seem they would almost have to be standing on each other's shoulders. You certainly don't have to shout to be heard there. If North Dakota were that densely populated we would have a population of about 48,000,000 people!

Over the years many people have asked me, "Why do you stay up north in that large refrigerated isolation booth?" (I know it's hard to believe, but that's the exact question they all asked.) Without really thinking about it I've always answered with the semi-intelligent, not well thought out answer of "Because". Now that I've really thought and talked about it, I've found there is no definitive answer. So now it seems an answer of "Because" really isn't that bad. I guess we all have reasons why we are where we are and almost every reason is different. This is how one transplanted North Dakotan felt:

"It was a strange and beautiful country my father had come to, so big and boundless he could look for miles out over the golden prairies and follow the unbroken horizon to where the midday blue met the bare peaks of the distant hills. No tree or bush to break the view, miles and miles of grass, acre after acre of waving grain, and, up above, God and that fiery chariot which beat remorselessly down upon a parched earth."

"The evenings brought also a greater, lonelier beauty. A crimson blue in the west marked the waning of the sun, the purple haze of the hills crept down to pursue the retreating glow and the whole world was hushed in peace."

"Now and then the silence was broken by the clear notes of a meadowlark on a nearby fence or the honk of wild geese far, far above, winging their way south."

"This was God's country. There was something in the stillness that spoke to Pop's soul, and he loved it."

A young black girl, who would become one of the greatest North Dakotans in the states short history, wrote those words many years ago. Her name was Era Bell Thompson. Her father brought her and the rest of his family to North Dakota in 1914 to get his family out of the city. Era Bell and her family first lived in the small eastern Burleigh County town of Driscoll, where Era Bell attended school from 1914 through the 1919-20 school year. They eventually moved to Bismarck, where she started to attend school in the fall of 1920. She graduated from Bismarck High School, where, even though she may have been able to get a part as a munchkin in the movie "The Wizard of Oz" (she was less than 5 feet tall), she starred on the track and basketball teams. Era Bell started her college education at UND (University of North Dakota) in 1925 where along with her studies she was also on the track team. While running track at UND she set 5 school records and matched 2 national records. After a couple years, she was forced to leave UND because of both her and her father's health problems. She eventually finished college, in 1932, at Morningside College in Sioux City, Iowa. Utilizing her natural writing talent and her college education, Era Bell began writing for Johnson Publishing, the publisher of Ebony magazine. In time she rose to the position of international editor with Ebony. She journeyed back to the Driscoll area many times to visit old friends, schoolmates, and neighbors. In fact, Driscoll is where her mother and three other family members are buried. Era Bell passed away in 1986. She's one of the most successful North Dakotans and is one of the recipients of the Teddy Roosevelt Roughrider Award. Yes, there are more.

Here are some more Teddy Roosevelt Roughrider Award winners. This award is the equivalent of being named to the North Dakota Hall of Fame. You should recognize a few of these names. At the top of the list is the person the award is named for:

Theodore Roosevelt was the 26th President of the United States. But before he was president, in the late 1800's he lived and ranched in southwestern North Dakota, where he became a legend. There he always demonstrated stamina, fairness, and perseverance. It's easy to see why he was elected President. The only national park in the state is named after him. Get a load of this name; the National Park Service named it the Theodore Roosevelt National Park. What imagination! They must have hired a New York 5th Avenue public relations firm to think that one up.

Roger Maris (1934-1985), Fargo, hit 61 home runs in 1961 to surpass the Major League Baseball single season home run record of the legendary Babe Ruth. The record was always controversial because Ruth hit 60 homeruns in a 154 game season, while Maris hit 61 in a 162 game season. At the least, Maris' record was for home runs in a 162 game season. Indeed, the commissioner of baseball at that time decreed that Maris' name in the record book would have an asterisk by it with a footnote saying that the 61 homers came in 162 games. Well, all baseball fans know that Maris' record has been surpassed a few times in the last few years. It seems the players that have surpassed it have all used some "performance enhancing" substances. It's just amazing, since the story broke about the use of these substances, the number of home runs dropped back down to what we consider normal in this "live ball" era. A coincidence! I think not! I think those players should all have an asterisk next to their names that refers to a comment that reads "chemically aided".

Louis L'Amour (1908-1988), Jamestown, was a tremendously prolific and popular western writer. Several of his books have been adapted to the movie screen, including my favorite western movie, "Conagher", starring my favorite actor, Sam Elliott, from the Louis L'Amour book with the same name. Other favorites are "The Sacketts" and "Crossfire Trail".

Phil Jackson (1942-), was born in Deer Lodge, Montana. His family moved to Williston, North Dakota during his youth. Phil played basketball at and graduated from high school in Williston and from college at the University of North Dakota in Grand Forks, where he was an All-American. He played in the NBA for the New York Knicks, where he was an important part of two NBA championship teams. His greatest claim to fame, however, is as a coach in the NBA, where he has matched the NBA record of the late great Boston Celtics coach Red Auerbach by coaching the Chicago Bulls and Los Angeles Lakers to a total of 9 NBA championships. In 2006, "the master of Zen", as he is referred to by sports reporters, (the Eastern Philosophy of Zen has had a big influence on his coaching philosophy) is still coaching in the NBA.

Angie Dickinson (1931-), Kulm, an actress who has had a long movie acting career, but is best known as Sgt. Suzanne "Pepper" Anderson in the TV series "Police Woman" that ran for 5 seasons in the 70's. In her younger years she guest starred on dozens of serial TV shows. She is still active; within the last year I watched an excellent movie "Pay It Forward" that she appeared in with Haley Joel Osment, Kevin Spacey and Helen Hunt.

Dorothy Stickney (1896-1998), Dickinson, an actress, who in 1971, in one of her last acting roles, played Emily Baldwin, one of the two Baldwin sisters in the made for TV movie "The Homecoming", a story about a Walton family Christmas. It was the pilot for the hit TV series, "The Waltons", that aired for nine seasons. You all know who the Waltons are don't you? I'm not talking about Sam and his kids, but about John Boy, Jim Bob, Jason, Elizabeth and the rest of that gang. The character that Dorothy played was also in the series but with a different actress in the role. Dorothy Stickney's acting career spanned 40 years from 1931 to her final performance in 1971.

Eric Sevareid (1912-1992), Velva, a journalist who was a contemporary of Edward R. Murrow and was known as one of "Murrow's Boys" during World War II. His Emmy and Peabody award winning 2-minute commentaries on CBS news earned him the nickname, "The Grey Eminence".

Peggy Lee (1922-2002), Jamestown, had her start as a big band singer with Benny Goodman in the 40's. She was best known for her "soft and cool" singing style. She was nominated for 12 Grammy Awards, winning a Grammy for her recording of "Is That All There Is?".

Larry Woiwode (1941-), Sykeston, who now lives near Mott, is North Dakota's poet laureate and an author who has sold over 2 million copies each of two of his books "Beyond the Bedroom Wall" and "What I'm Going To Do, I Think".

Warren Christopher (1925-), Scranton, served as Assistant US Secretary of State in the Carter administration and as the US Secretary of State in the Clinton administration.

Rev. Richard Halverson (1916-1995), Pingree, served as the Chaplain of the US Senate from 1981-1994.

Harry Pearce (1942-), Bismarck, served as Chairman of the Board for General Motors Corporation for 5 years, retiring from that post in 2001. Originally was hired as General Counsel for GM.

The people listed above are about a third of those who have received the Roughrider Award. There are a total of 35 Roughrider Award winners. They are among the best and brightest when it comes to North Dakotans. But wait, I'm going to throw out a few more names and bios. Have you heard of any of these people? Here are some more of us that are or were in the sports and entertainment industries:

Rick Helling, Lakota via Fargo (Milwaukee Brewers), **Travis Hafner,** Sykeston (Cleveland Indians) and **Darin Erstad,** Jamestown (Los Angeles Angels) are current Major League baseball players. Helling currently pitches for the Brewers. He was drafted in the first round by Texas and had a 20-win season for the Rangers early in his career. Travis Hafner is one of the bright rising stars in the league. Given the nickname "Pronk" (a combination of Project and Donkey) by his teammates, he is the Indian's best hitter. Late in the 2006 season, he was second in the American League in home runs with 42 and RBI's with 117. Also this season he hit 6 grand slam home runs, which tied the single season record of ex-New York Yankee great, Don Mattingly. His season ended a few weeks early when he broke a finger as the result of being hit in the hand by a pitch in September. Erstad has played his entire career for the LA Angels and was a valuable member of the Angels 2002 world championship team. Darin is one of only two players (Robin Yount is the other) to win Gold Gloves as both an infielder and an outfielder.

Ann Sothern, Valley City, actress, was beautiful and successful. She was nominated for a Best Supporting Actress Academy Award for her performance in her final film "The Whales of August" in 1987. She was also a great friend of and acted in sitcoms with the legendary Lucille Ball. She had a 60-year acting career, first performing in 1927.

Lynn Anderson, born in Grand Forks, is a popular country singer. Her career really took off when she recorded (and won a Grammy for) the crossover country/pop hit, "I Never Promised You A Rose Garden" in 1970. Before she recorded that song she was a regular for a season on the "Lawrence Welk Show". Her mother is the great country songwriter, Liz Anderson.

Dale Brown, Minot, is remembered most as the coach that recruited Shaquille O'Neal when Brown was head basketball coach at Louisiana State University. O'Neal is currently the center for the reigning NBA champion Miami Heat and was the center for Phil Jackson and the Los Angeles Lakers when they won three NBA titles.

Shadoe Stevens, Jamestown, was host of radio's "America's Top Forty" for many years and is currently hosting "The Worlds Top 30". A deejay by trade, he has also served as an announcer for several TV shows, including the game show "Hollywood Squares" for much of its history.

See, you do know someone from North Dakota!

It looks like being related to a famous North Dakotan had very little pull with mid 19th century Native Americans. Louis L'Amour's great-grandfather, Lt. Ambrose Freeman, was killed in North Dakota in the summer of 1863. Freeman was part of the force that General Sibley led into North Dakota to punish the Sioux tribes involved in the Minnesota Massacre of 1862. He was killed during the time that Sibley's forces and the Sioux were fighting the Battle of Big Mound in what is now northern Kidder County. Freeman was not actually killed in the battle. Gen. Sibley had issued orders to the effect that no one should separate from the main body for any reason. Lt. Freeman disobeyed orders and went hunting. He was killed while hunting of all things.

Who am I? I am just another one of those kids born in the midst of the great post World War II baby boom. I am the third of six kids of a farmer-mechanic of German heritage and a little red haired freckle faced homemaker-sales clerk of English-Norwegian ancestry. It was my good fortune to grow up in Steele, a small town in the heart of North Dakota. I'm sure you're thinking "Good fortune?" I can hear the snickering from here, but as they say in classical literature, "Beauty is in the eye of the beholder". I spent my childhood years living in Steele. When I was in high school we moved to a farm just outside of town, where my folks still live. My family actually reversed the trend of leaving the farm for the city. That was pretty rare and I can only think of one or two other instances of that happening in the Steele area community.

In the USA people from our generation are called "Boomers". Even in North Dakota there are lots of us. Because of us, almost every small town school's enrollment spiked during the late 60's to the early 70's. Those were the golden years of rural small town America and small town schools.

So what do we do here in North Dakota? North Dakota is best known for its agricultural products, but if you look at how much outmigration there is and just who it is that's leaving, it appears that North Dakota's finest product has been it's young people. The kids grow up, receive their elementary and secondary education and many of them go to college here. But then the realities set in for a good portion of the young men and women. They start leaving the state for a number of reasons. Some will just never be satisfied living in North Dakota and leave for the brighter lights. As for the kids that would prefer to stay, when they finish school and enter the job force, if their plans include raising a family, they may have a problem. You see, lack of jobs isn't the problem here. There are all kinds of 9, 10 or 11 dollar per hour jobs but you can't raise a family on those wages. If your choice is to be a professional like a lawyer, engineer, CPA, psychologist or any other given line of professional work, with our small population, the opportunities are most likely few and the competition for those jobs intense. So it may be that their only alternative is to leave the state. In most groups of graduates, relationships and marriages also take some out of state. My high school class was no exception, as many as 40% of my classmates have left, for one or more of the reasons listed. They've scattered all over the country, but it seems like the main recipients of North Dakota's young people are the neighboring states of Minnesota and Montana and also Colorado, with Minnesota's Minneapolis/St. Paul and Washington state's Seattle as the top metro destinations. A lot of them that leave have the notion in the back of their mind that some day they'll return to that peaceful place up north, their prairie home. If they're lucky, they find a way.

North Dakota kids make intelligent, hardworking, and reliable employees. I'm not just saying that because you can't disprove it. All you need to do is ask the personnel manager of any company in the Minneapolis metro area what he or she thinks of North Dakota young people and he or she will tell you same thing. With traits like these, North Dakota youth are prime candidates for work forces all across the country.

I've been told that North Dakota's young ladies are held in such high regard as childcare providers that well to do East Coast families, looking for a summer nanny, will hire them on the spot if they can produce a North Dakota driver's license. A couple of young ladies I went to high school with each spent a summer working as a nanny in Connecticut, one to the kids of the since deceased singer Harry Chapin (of "Cats in the Cradle" fame).

North Dakota is well known for its cultural diversity (Native Americans, German-Russians, Norwegians, etc), but has never really been a destination for more than just a few black people, especially early in the 20th century. When Era Bell Thompson's family lived in the Driscoll area, there were a couple other black families that were farming near Steele. Their last name was Johnson. Era Bell noted that the three black families got together a few times on holidays, and when they did, a large percentage of North Dakota's black people were gathered under one roof. So that gives you a rough idea of the numbers of blacks in the state at that time. I think the official census number for 1910 or 20 was something like 400 blacks in North Dakota, most of them homesteaders.

If you didn't know it before, you've learned it by reading this, that North Dakota is a very small state population wise. We have a very low crime rate and terrorists are about as common as white buffalo. To those of you that are lacking in knowledge of buffalo, white buffalo are very rare, and because they were so rare, were considered sacred by the native Americans. So, because terrorists are non-existent, state officials can pretty much go where they desire. They move about to appearances and meetings unencumbered by security personnel. In times of stress that require security (such as following the 9-11 terror attacks), a state trooper or two may be assigned to the governor.

The governor lives in an unguarded house on the capitol grounds, where kids can go and knock on the door on Halloween and the chances are good that the state's first lady or the governor will answer the knock. If you see the governor and/or his family out and about, you'll notice he's pretty much on his own when he's off duty. It's much the same when he's on duty. This is North Dakota, what could happen? There just isn't a whole lot of danger out here.

Let's just say for the purpose of discussion, someone abducts the governor and holds him for ransom. He isn't privy to any national secrets. He's not a wealthy man. What could the kidnappers gain from the situation? What would they demand? Two pigs and a steer so they can make some sausage? 100 pounds of potatoes and a tear drop ham, so they can make a few dozen lefse and a batch or two of klubb? Okay, I can see that maybe the lefse might be a logical reason to abduct him. You'd have to carefully weigh the gain against the consequences. Let's see, lefse; 10 years in prison, lefse; 10 years in prison, lefse; 10 years in prison. Wow, that's a close call! I'm leaning toward the lefse (if my wife makes it), it's only 10 years in prison. (Those of us that love lefse understand that a situation like this could create quite a quandary. If you don't know what lefse is, it's a Norwegian delicacy. More later.)

While our previous governor, Ed Schafer was in office; I sat and talked politics him several times while getting dressed after a workout at a local health club. Our lockers were right beside each other. That was fun, I really appreciated the opportunity to talk with him, and I'm sure he thought it was just great to be able to converse with a stranger and not feel threatened.

It may come as a shock to you to hear this, but we're not exactly in the main stream of society out here. Partly because of our isolation and partly because there are so few of us, we do have a lot of freedoms. When we were growing up, the biggest thing we had to worry about was keeping the furrow straight while we were plowing. We've got the freedom to never worry about traffic jams. We very rarely worry about home break ins. We've got the freedom to park our car almost anywhere. We've got the freedom to get out of town in 5 minutes. We've got the freedom to send our kids outside or to school without worry. We've got the freedom to leave our house door unlocked. We've got the freedom to walk down the street at night. We don't have to worry about being car jacked. Our commute to work is a freedom; we're not held hostage for the hours it takes some to commute. For most of

Ken Stein

the people here it's about 15 minutes or less a day. We don't have to stay inside on a bad smog day because we have no bad smog days. We could go on all day about our freedoms. I'm not going to sit here and try to get you to believe there is no crime, because that wouldn't be true, because there is some, not much, but there is some. But it really is as quiet and safe a place as there is. I don't think we ever really appreciate how free we are, we tend to take it for granted. Freedom in North Dakota is not elusive, it's aways there waiting for you when you walk out the door or get out of bed in the morning.

Before we go any further, we have to make something very important crystal clear. Although I never personally experienced any problems, I'm not so naïve as to think that there were or are no incidents of infringements on our personal freedoms such as spousal abuse, child abuse, or incest in North Dakota. Sadly those things are inherent in the human race, partly because of social and economic conditions, partly because they are a learned behavior and partly just because there are some mean SOB's out there. I remember an incident of spousal and child abuse in my home county. It involved a very courageous wife and mother who valued her children's lives above her own. Disregarding the consequences to herself, she shot and killed her abusive spouse. She was arrested by county authorities, was charged with a crime and brought to trial. The district court jury decided that she had acted in self-defense and found her innocent of the charges brought against her. Her husband clearly got what he deserved. Western justice.

So you see, North Dakotans are in fact, only human, but we're really a pretty darn good bunch of people. If you were to take a walk down a street of a small town in North Dakota, what would the people be like that you bumped into? Being male, I can only speak for the males. The typical North Dakotan is fairly conservative, but he's not going to preach to you. He considers himself a Republican, but can't explain why the whole North Dakota Congressional delegation is Democratic. He likes the actor Johnny Depp…. but only in the movies. Johnny is too Hollywood for him. His favorite Hollywood type is someone like Tom Hanks or Harrison Ford, someone you wouldn't mind having over for a barbecue or a beer. He thinks there should be a John Wayne and/or Clint Eastwood movie channel on cable. He's married to a North Dakota girl. He's at least an average or above husband and father. Beer is his beverage of choice. He will watch a rodeo occasionally, but he's not a cowboy. He's more likely to be found at a junior high or high school sporting event watching as his kids participate. He played two or more sports in high school and considers himself athletic. He drives a four-wheel drive pickup, not because it's fashionable, but because he needs it. He probably learned to drive a tractor before he was interested in girls. He owns more than one gun. He is fairly well educated, usually beyond high school. He is most likely much more educated than his parents are. He would be very happy if his daughter brought a North Dakota boy home to meet her parents, but is open minded enough to carefully consider his daughters feelings before forming an opinion. The chances are very good he is of Norwegian or German-Russian heritage. He has no idea what the second and third forks are for at a formal dinner setting let alone the second and third wineglasses, but he loves a fine meal. The chances are better than even that he grew up on a farm. He's a rabid Minnesota Viking or Green Bay Packer fan, one or the other, but not both. He's a rabid North Dakota State University Bison or University of North Dakota Fighting Sioux fan, one or the other, but not both. He may have attended one of the two larger state universities. He seldom uses the sick leave he accumulates at work. If he is a farmer, during planting or harvesting season there is no such thing as being sick. He takes a lot of pride in his work whether it is farming, building tractors, or selling insurance. He will sit and watch a beautiful sunset and has watched the sun rise maybe hundreds, or even thousands of times. And oh yeah, he loves the outdoors. If you live in North Dakota, it's never far away.

As we started to say earlier before we were sidetracked, the production of agricultural commodities has always been the mainstay of North Dakota's economy. The only area of production that could challenge that status is energy. We use surplus corn to make ethanol, surplus sunflower oil to make biodiesel, wind generation of electricity, coal fired generation of electricity, hydroelectric power, conversion of coal to gaseous and liquid fuels, and of course production of oil and natural gas make up most of the energy sector. All of this energy production has the state on the verge of becoming a major player in the energy business. But farming is still the state's bread and butter.

Farming itself has evolved so much over the years. Farming used to be a simple process of plowing and putting seed into the ground, and when the grain grew up and the seeds ripened, harvesting it. Not any more! Now, for instance, if you raise malting barley, you specifically try to raise low protein (You actually want the protein in an ideal range of 9-12.5 %) barley, with 75 % or better plump kernels, so that it can be used for making beer. If you raise feed barley, you want high protein and plumpness doesn't matter. You also need to manipulate the amount of available nitrogen that you apply either as urea or anhydrous ammonia to get maximum yield. Raising wheat, canola, flax, sunflowers and any other grain also present challenges unique to each particular seed.

Just what is all the stuff that we grow in North Dakota used for? Most of it is for animal or people food. Barley is mostly used to make beer (or as beer is lovingly referred to in beer drinking circles, Vitamin B) and to feed livestock. Corn is used to make ethanol, to feed livestock and for human food products like corn flakes, corn itself, and tortillas to name a few. Canola and sunflowers are crushed for cooking oils.

Durum wheat is used to make pasta, while spring wheat is ground for the flour used in baking. Flax is used to make linseed oil and it's straw is used to make linen. Oats are used to feed livestock and for human food products. Soybeans are used for soy oil and a myriad of food products. Peas ands other beans are raised for human consumption and some peas are fed to livestock.

The equipment on the modern farm is incredible. We certainly have made major advancements since the turn of the century homesteading days. The farmers use air seeders to seed directly into standing stubble. With one pass they can apply seed, fertilizer and nitrogen accurately, at the exact rate desired. The name air seeder says it all. It uses compressed air to meter out the seed and fertilizer using what are called Venturi manifolds. Are you familiar with that law in physics known as the Venturi effect, you know the one based on Bernoulli's principle? Of course we all know that one! In simple terms, the principle says that if you blow a stream of compressed air into a tube with a constriction, a vacuum will be created downstream from that constriction. The variables affecting the amount of vacuum created are the compressed air pressure and the size of the constriction. So you suck up seed and fertilizer to be distributed with the vacuum created in the previously mentioned Venturi manifolds. Nitrogen uses its own delivery system, separate from the air seeder. It comes compressed as anhydrous ammonia, so it is metered out using that compression as the driving force. The air seeder also incorporates seed and fertilizer into the soil so it has to dig up the soil as well as meter out the seed and fertilizer. An air seeder can be 36 feet wide or wider. A four-wheel drive tractor with a lot of horsepower is required to pull it because a 36 foot air seeder that plants a row about every 6-8 inches has to dig up a lot of dirt. The tractor can also be guided by GPS (Global Positioning System) technology. GPS can be used to physically control the tractor. GPS technology also allows you to pinpoint areas where you want to apply more or less fertilizer or seed, where there are rocks to move and it is very useful for calculating accurately your planted acreage for each crop you grow.

The combines (grain harvesters) that are used to harvest the grain have integrated moisture and yield analyzers. You need to know the moisture content of the grain when it is harvested because each type of grain has a safe storage moisture level. If it's at or below that level it can then be safely stored for future use. The grain harvester is called a combine because it is a combination of two machines, the binder and the thresher. They can also use GPS technology and the newest machines can eat up acres of grain like crazy. They are the biggest machines you'll see on a farm.

Today's farmer just about has to have a degree in chemistry, so he can understand how to use all the agricultural chemicals. He will have to mix herbicides to control combinations of annual grasses and broadleaf weeds. He can and carefully will use herbicides that kill all vegetation when doing no-till summer fallow. He will have to use fungicides in the treatment of numerous crop diseases. He has to be able to identify insect pests and then use the proper insecticides to control them. He needs to understand global positioning technology, long term weather forecasting and global economics. He has to be aware of trends in diets in countries all over the world. It's not just putting seeds in the ground anymore. So if someone tells you he is just a farmer, you'll know better. He's a lot more than 'just a farmer'.

On the down side of the farming business, with rising land and crop input costs and weather that is very inconsistent, net farming income from year to year can vary tremendously. Because of these uncertainties, the number of young people staying on the farms is very low in many areas. This is especially true in the western two-thirds of North Dakota. The costs associated with a young person starting to farm completely from scratch are incredibly high. Unless that person inherits land it is almost impossible today.

In the last few years, we have seen a new dilemma that farmers are facing in western North Dakota. The dilemma is that land costs are being driven up by non-local outdoorsmen who are buying up a lot of the land that's for sale at higher than market prices. The buyers are generally buying the land to hunt on. Local farmers say they can't afford to buy land at these inflated prices. The nonresident hunters say they are trying to avoid paying trespass fees and 'no hunting' signs. And the farmers still say the local hunters are the bad guys! Many times they are. The local hunters make their own bed and so have to lie in it. Too many of them assume "No Hunting" signs are meant for someone else and ignore them. The landowner usually has a very good reason for posting his land and even if he doesn't, it's his land to do with as he pleases.

There is a book with the title "Buffalo Commons", written by an east-coast couple, Drs. Frank and Deb Popper. They were at Rutgers University in 1987 when it was published. The book states that because of the uncertainty of farm economics and a dearth of young farmers, that portions of the Great Plains will eventually revert back to a "Buffalo Commons" (it's natural state). It was, of course, ridiculed out on the plains when it was released. But, if we take an honest look at the situation, almost anyone would have to say the chances are better than even, that at the very least, some of their predictions will come true. In some thinly populated areas of North Dakota, such as west of Highway 52 and north of Highway 2 in northwest North Dakota, in the not too distant future we may begin to see some of the poorer farmland and pasture actually abandoned. This area is very lightly populated and 20 years from now when the current population of farmers is gone, the replacements for them will be far fewer in number. There will be an abundance of land for each to farm, so they can afford to become a little choosy. The counties may eventually become one of their own larger landowners when they assume ownership of unused land in lieu of back taxes.

In North Dakota today, there are many small towns that are rapidly dying. The numbers of babies being born in many of these rural and semi-rural areas are very low. Why? It's certainly not because of a lack of sex drive, but because there are no longer many couples in their childbearing years in these areas.

So, what's going to happen to small town North Dakota? Most of the small towns that are cut off from major highways and railroads will wither away and die. If you look at a road map you can almost predict which towns will not survive. If the town is not on an active railroad, or a major highway and 50 or more miles from one of the major towns, it's chances of surviving are not too good. Today in Bismarck and maybe to a much lesser extent in Fargo, when you meet someone and ask them where they're from, probably more than half will name a small town somewhere in the area. They are leaving those small towns in droves. Unless the small towns are particularly aggressive in recruiting a savior that will bring jobs, there's nothing they can do to prevent it. Even farm support businesses will not be immune. Farmers can easily deal directly with suppliers and buyers and don't need local middlemen. Centrally located equipment dealers haul broken down equipment off the farm to their shop and back again by truck. So what is there to keep the towns alive? Absolutely nothing. When the current population ages and passes on, that will be it.

There is normally only about 2.5% unemployment in North Dakota. The government says that with that low a rate everyone that wants to work here has already got a job. Why won't people move in from out of state if there are so many jobs? Until the state government and the employers recognize that they are losing a battle for workers with other states that won't happen. There are two reasons North Dakota is losing that battle. First, while the cost of living in North Dakota is lower (mainly due to housing costs) than the coastal states, it is probably the highest in the west north central region. Second, Labor Department statistics show that the average median wage in the west north central region is about 13-15% lower than the national average. That's two strikes against North Dakota. The main reason for working here is quality of life, something that is not so apparent to someone who doesn't live here.

North Dakota is a "right to work state" a philosophy that decreases the influence of labor unions and makes North Dakota an attractive target for a potential employer who is determined to keep labor costs down and profits high. If you were someone looking for a job you would have to be pretty desperate to, in affect, take as much as a 15% pay cut (not to mention the high cost of living) to come here. Recently a restaurant in Bismarck had to close because it couldn't find employees. If you were to examine Job Service files you would discover that it is not only the food service industry that is scrambling for employees, but the health care industry is also struggling, as are a lot of employers in other businesses and industries.

Just recently, I heard a radio commercial touting a job that paid $11 an hour with some benefits on top of the salary. The ad made it sound like this job was the answer to anyone's dream of being successful. Well I hope no one went into that job thinking they were in tall cotton. This is a prime example of the low wage job that is all too common in North Dakota. If you do a little math, you quickly see this is about $23,000 per year, before taxes. Even If you're single, it's tough to live comfortably on that, unless your employer provides health insurance.

But all is not lost, most towns and cities on North Dakotas two main east-west highways, I-94 and US2 and in the corridor along the north south I-29 are surviving. In a lot of instances they are thriving, especially the four biggest towns of Fargo (not the movie, the town), Bismarck, Minot (Why not Minot?), and Grand Forks and also the small towns near them. The Fargo and Grand Forks areas in the east with more stable weather, higher population and higher value dry land crop production (beets, beans, etc) are certainly in a good position to grow. Minot will live or die depending on the fate of the Air Force base north of town. Bismarck has a growing population and is striving mightily to create new job opportunities, with mixed success. The huge number of jobs associated with state government is what really fuels Bismarck's economy.

In those larger towns a middle class of blue-collar workers and young professionals is rapidly developing that will become a political force. Although a lot of the denizens of the bigger towns have rural roots, they are already having an affect on state and local politics as the conservative views of their parents moderate in these young urban middle class North Dakotans. There is a very good chance that North Dakota will become a more liberal thinking and voting state as it becomes less rural.

There are a few small towns that have something unique going on and they seem to be bucking the trends. Carrington has a highly successful pasta plant. Garrison has Lake Sakakawea and its tourism. Washburn, Center, Underwood, Beulah and Hazen are in the heart of Coal Country. New England has the states women's prison. Tioga is in the middle of the new oil boom. Those are a few of the lucky ones.

But that's enough of my philosophy. It's sad for me to see the towns dying that I was so familiar with in my youth, but I'm afraid it's just natural selection. It's the evolution of our towns and the survival of the fittest. I'm afraid my roots are very deep in rural North Dakota.

CHAPTER 2

MY HOMETOWN

My family has been in south central North Dakota in the neighborhood of a hundred years. The maternal side arrived in 1905 when Great grandfather Henry homesteaded northeast of Driscoll in Clear Lake Township of Burleigh County. The paternal side arrived in Kidder County in 1915 when Great grandfather August bought a farm in western Kidder County, northwest of Steele in Pleasant Hill Township.

The main push to populate the area east of Bismarck took place during a 30-year period at the end of the 19th century and the beginning of the 20th century. Steele was founded at the beginning of that period in 1881. Not so coincidentally, the Northern Pacific railroad reached south central North Dakota a few years before that in 1872. The siding that would become Steele was used by the railroad as a water replenishment site for their steam locomotives. The founder of Steele, whose name was Wilbur F. Steele, had hoped that the state capital would be established at Steele when North Dakota achieved statehood. He built what became the county courthouse in 1883. The building was originally intended to be used as a hotel to house state legislators. Wilbur eventually lost the capitol derby and the capitol was established 40 miles west in Bismarck. Sometime shortly after his failure to make Steele the state capitol, Mr. Steele sold the hotel building to the county. It was in 1885 that the county took over the building as the county's center of government. He had constructed the building at a cost of $25,000, and it was sold to the county at the bargain price of $20,000. It originally was a three story building, but several years after the county bought it, a leaking roof was repaired, the third story was removed and also the entrance was moved from the north side to its present south side location.

Wilbur Steele left the area shortly after failing to make Steele the state capital. While in the Dakotas he had also served two years in the Lower House of the territorial legislature. He died a poor man in New York City in 1917, having lost most of his money in a failed investment scheme.

Mr. Steele built a farmstead on the east side of Steele, intending it to be used as a demo farm, to help attract new settlers. I believe the original barn still stands today. He also built a very fine house on the farm. Years later, shortly after the turn of the century, the local banker, Mr. John Robinson, moved the house into town, and lived in it until his death in 1926. At some point after that it became known as the Dornacker house. It still stood on the north side of town when I was young. I do remember being in it before it was torn down. It was literally a mansion. It was very impressive by today's standards, and I'll bet in 1885 it knocked their socks off. It was torn down over 30 years ago to make room for some apartments. My Grandma Ida worked in the Steele house when she cleaned for Mr. Robinson right around 1920, before she married Grandpa August.

While in Steele, Mr. Steele also constructed a brick factory that utilized local clay as its raw material. Those bricks were used to build the courthouse and other vintage buildings in Steele. He built a spur line from the Northern Pacific main line to the brick factory. He named it the Steele-Alaska Northwestern railroad. He printed up passes for free travel on his railroad and exchanged them with owners of real railroads.

They discovered his hoax and called him to a meeting. At the meeting he boasted to the actual railroad owners that although his railroad was shorter than any other was, it was just as wide as any! There is one other connection in the area to the Steele family. My Dad grew up on the shores of a lake southeast of Steele named Lake Etta. That Lake Etta was named for Wilbur Steele's wife Etta. Rumor has it that Mrs. Steele used to sail a small sailboat on it.

Steele's greatest claim to fame unfortunately no longer lives in town. Steele was, for many years, the home of the family of Dick Clark's wife, Kari. Clark was the longtime host of "American Bandstand", and hosted the New Years celebration show "New Years Rockin Eve" for many years. When Kari's family moved into town, she was already in college. Kari only lived in Steele during the summers while she was in college. She taught dance in Steele during those summers. I do remember taking ballroom dancing lessons from her. You'd never believe that if you watched me try to dance now. I went to school with Kari's brother and her two sisters.

All of the kids have long since moved away and Kari's mom passed away a year or so ago. When the family lived in Steele, Dick and Kari were fairly frequent visitors. They were the grand marshals of the parade during Steele's centennial celebration held in 1981. They were always very passive visitors, trying hard to not make waves. Although Dick could have bought and sold Steele with his pocket change, you would have sworn he was not wealthy. He and Kari would often go grocery shopping for Esther when they were in Steele. You would have thought that he was just a local guy. The only tip off was his hair. It just didn't look like a Ray Schneider haircut (Who is Ray Schneider? Keep reading!). It was pretty rare to see a real hairstyle like Dick's in Steele. Incidentally, my most vivid memory of Dick Clark in Steele was on a very windy day. Dick was standing outside the grocery store when I happened to drive by. Like I said it was very windy and not a hair on his head was moving. His hairspray must have had phenomenal holding power.

So who is Ray Schneider? In Steele, we had a barber, Ray, who just passed away this year, who cut my hair when I was a youngster 45 years ago. Ray was one of the real nice people in this world. But, Ray was a barber, not a hair stylist. I do remember the haircuts Ray gave; they were all the same. I'd better clarify that; he did have two different cuts, the 'regular' cut that I got and the 'flattop' cut my Dad got. You could request any type of cut you wanted, as long as it was a regular cut or a flat top. So you did have a choice! When you got a haircut from Ray it was always a work of art, always perfectly done. If you were a teenager his 'regular' cut was just a little short for most of us. So, if you wanted your hair to look nice for something special, you just went in a little early and by our standards it would look fine when your event rolled around. But there are a lot of heartbroken men who will no longer be able to get their hair cut by Ray after nearly 45 years. I don't think anyone will move into town to replace him. Those guys won't know what to do, the beauty shop girls will ask them how they want their haircut and they won't know what to tell them. Maybe they are going to offer a "Ray Schneider special." Ray is a Steele legend.

Let's change gears a little and I'll tell you all about a true story of murder and vengeance. After all, at the turn of the century western North Dakota was still on the frontier. Steele was the site of one of the last vigilante hangings in North Dakota. It took place in 1912 shortly after George Baker murdered his wife, Myrtle, and her father, Thomas Glass, in Dawson. Myrtle had left her husband, taken their two children and moved back to her father's home in Dawson. Glass was a well-known and respected local pioneer, so the crime really shocked the community, so much so that they took up arms to settle it themselves. Shortly after the murders were committed, Baker was arrested and locked up in the

Kidder County jail in Steele. Glass' friends conspired to take things into their own hands. They became Baker's judge, jury and also his executioner, and to that end, shortly after he was jailed, a fairly large group of masked men, presumably from Dawson, took George Baker from his cell. They drug him down the street to the railroad stockyards. There they hung him on the cross member over the stockyard's front gate and leaving nothing to chance, they also shot him, and so executed him for the murders of Myrtle Baker and Thomas Glass.

In our small town America, everyone knows all the kids, heck they even know all the dogs. You don't come to a small town in North Dakota to disappear. If someone tries, they quickly find they stand out like a sore thumb. A lot of people that move in from outside the area realize fairly soon just how good a place this is and they never want to leave. That will even happen to some big city born and bred people. But on the other side of the coin, many can't shake the feelings of isolation and they leave after a short stay. There have been several attempts to lure people from out of state to small towns by giving them, free of charge, lots to build homes on. In attempting to do that, what they have found out is, as I said earlier in this paragraph, is that they either love living here and stay, or hate it and leave. There is very little middle ground. Either way while they're here, they won't find better hospitality anywhere than that shown to them by their North Dakota neighbors. There was a case worth noting in Robinson, one of our small Kidder County towns. A couple moved to Robinson from Philadelphia. They loved it there and they tried for a year and a half to find jobs that would reimburse them anywhere near what they made in Philadelphia. They finally gave up on their dream and moved back to Pennsylvania because they couldn't find an employer who would pay them what they were worth.

Back in the late 50's to around 1960, a movie theater, the Roxy, was still operating in Steele. What was it with the word

Roxy? Why were so many theaters named 'the Roxy'? Well, I just happen to know! In 1927 a man (and a sometime actor) by the name of Samuel L. Rothapfel built a 6000 seat theater in New York. His stage name was actually "Roxy" and so he called his theater "Roxy's". New York in those days was the center of the universe more or less. This was quite early in the movie business, so theaters were few but the numbers were growing fast. Other theater owners in other cities, wanting to mimic New York, used the name "Roxy" for their theaters also. Today the word "Roxy" has almost become a synonym for "movie theater", both here and in many countries abroad, especially England. You don't think I knew that off the top of my head do you? Thank heaven for the internet. Anyway, I remember going to Saturday matinees almost every weekend. We had tickets that allowed us to go to more than one matinee and they were punched every time we went in. There was nothing like a theater full of kids on a Saturday afternoon. There was a lot of cheering for the hero and booing of the villain. We got pretty excited. But sadly, the era of small town movie theaters was nearly over. Movie theaters in small towns are very rare these days, probably because of the high cost per showing of modern movies. One day a big truck came, they jacked up the Roxy, slid some big timbers underneath it and hauled the building away to become the county shop. That was a very inglorious ending for a great building. Shortly after that, they started to build a new building that turned out to be a bowling alley. A new form of entertainment had arrived in this small town, but it was for older kids and adults. The little kids missed the Roxy. Today the bowling alley is no longer in use either. It is the victim of a combination of an aging population and high maintenance costs. When the bowling alley first opened, they did offer a Youth Bowling League. In those days there were almost twice as many kids as there are today. There are still enough kids, but young people today have a lot of other interests, including more and more sophisticated video games.

When I was a kid, the distinction between church and state was not nearly as well defined as it is today. Back then the schools as well as the churches put on real Christmas programs. One of the big things that we anticipated all year long was that after both the school and church programs, each kid was given a fairly large bag that contained Christmas candy, unshelled peanuts and other nuts and maybe an apple or orange. Looking back, I think the bags of goodies were a bribe to help get us to put on the programs. I don't know what they were called, but my favorite treats were dome shaped candies that had a white inside and a chocolate outside. I haven't seen any of them for years. In today's world public schools aren't allowed to put on programs that celebrate the birth of anyone with any stronger religious connotations than Donald Duck. In a public school, religion is a no-no, according to our courts.

When we were kids, the Kidder County Fall Fair was a very big deal. The fair is still in existence, but is held in the summer. As it's original name implies, years ago, it was actually held in the fall (September) not late summer. They used to have a full-blown carnival in town as well as the stock and produce shows. I remember one year we talked Dad into getting on one of the really wild rides. We never did find his pliers that he always carried in his pants pliers' pocket. The carnival was not just rides but also had a midway with games of chance and curiosity shows. We got out of school on the Friday of that week so we could take more of it in. Today the county fair is just a very dim shadow of its former self. It's too bad; it was one of the highlights of our year.

In 50's and 60's most small towns had a local doctor. Our local doctor was our neighbor when I was a kid. He was a Ukrainian immigrant. I'm not sure if he and his wife fled the Nazis or the communists. Anyway, whoever it was, their loss was our gain. He shepherded me through broken arms, childhood diseases, and believe it or not, a pitchfork through one of my legs. His favorite line when you were making an official visit to him was, "We give you shot". There wasn't a kid in town who didn't use that line at some point in their playtime. If you say those words today to any longtime Steele resident, you'll get a chuckle. In the 50's and 60's, going to the doctor didn't require taking out a second mortgage on the house. Those were the days when doctors like Dr. Zukowsky, who were immigrants, were happy to be part of the community and lived modestly. Mostly, they were just happy to be in America. But this isn't the 50's and 60's anymore! With today's huge malpractice insurance rates, government mandates and regulations, and the costs associated with completing the course of study to become a doctor, medical spending is going out of sight. Depending on the school, you can spend in the hundreds of thousands of dollars to get MD or DO next to your name. We used to get patched up by the local doctor for a few bucks or a chicken. Those days have passed. Now we have an 'industry' to birth babies, sew up cuts, and put casts on broken limbs.

In the 20's and 30's, my Dad and his brother and sisters were born at the Karpen birthing house in Steele, with a midwife tending to Grandma. Cost was less than $100 each. Today the costs associated with bringing a baby into the world, mostly because of the reasons outlined earlier, are in the many thousands of dollars. On the other hand, it's not like there haven't been tremendous and amazing improvements made in medicine. Babies live and thrive today that wouldn't have had a prayer back in the days when my Dad was born. Medicine is similar to the auto industry. How could that be? Not too long ago someone made the comment to me that "they don't make cars like they used to", to which I replied "Thank goodness for that!" Thank goodness the practice of medicine isn't what it used to be.

You're going to want to know, so I'd better tell the story of the pitchfork through my leg. I'd like to be able to tell you the circumstances were that I was defending myself in a desperate battle with cattle thieves and I took one for the Gipper or something adventurous like that. But it wasn't nearly so interesting. All I was doing was cleaning up some loose hay upstairs in the barn. There were a few small square bales in amongst the loose hay. I was swinging the fork down and back to move hay to my rear. (It seemed easier than pushing it, but maybe a little dangerous?) The fork just bounced off a bale, deflected toward me and a tine went through my leg. I think I had a legitimate excuse. At that time I probably qualified as a "city kid" because we hadn't been on the farm for very long, so I didn't know any better. See, the story was pretty blasé.

Our little town also had a resident dentist until the early 70's. You've heard of the Don Knotts movie, "The Shakiest Gun in the West" haven't you? Well, Doc Needham wasn't quite as shaky as Don Knotts in that movie, but he wasn't exactly "Cool hand Luke" either. He was a good dentist and did a real nice job, but he would scare the crap out of you if you didn't know him.

Many of North Dakota's small towns are still great places to raise and educate kids, depending on the proximity of good school facilities. Steele is one of the best. Why? Steele has a new high school, replacing the 85 years old structure we came of age in. It is complete with updated shop and music facilities. The school also has very good athletic fields. They are all part of a recreation complex built in the late seventies by a private group, the local park board and the school district. The football, track, and baseball fields are the school district's to use and maintain. The football field is at least a hundred times better than the bare dirt that we played football on. You can still see the scar on my hand where I cut it on an old beer or pop can that was crushed into the dirt of the old football field. When you fell or were tackled on the old field the ground hurt worse than the tackler did. With all these great facilities in place, Steele-Dawson is well situated to be the last school in

Kidder County. Very soon there will only be two high schools in the county, at Tappen and at Steele. Already the Tappen school is less than half the size (in numbers of students) of Steele's school.

So how did we boomers affect the local school enrollments? Right now in Steele, there are about 275 kids total in K-12 for an average of about 21 per grade. If we compare that number to the total number of students in 1970 you'll get a good idea of just how many boomers there were in the North Dakota school systems. It's pretty amazing! In 1970, Steele had 515 students in K-12, with a largest class of 52 students. There were almost 40 kids per grade! That's almost double the current average grade size. On top of that, when we started school we were all packed into the old high school building. It wasn't until about 1965 that Steele's current elementary wing was completed and we were finally able to spread out a little.

While Steele is holding it's own as far as numbers of students enrolled, things are not so rosy up in northern Kidder County. A little investigating there reveals some startling numbers. The Kidder County towns in the north include Pettibone (population 80), Lake Williams (population < 20?), Robinson (population 66) and Tuttle (population 96). There are two elementary schools and one high school. The one high school is in Tuttle and has 49 students, while the two elementary schools have a total of only 23 students. For them, the writing is on the wall. The high school will rapidly decrease in size when the current high school classes graduate. It's hard for a high school to properly teach kids when there are so few there. To be honest, some of the parents in these towns that are closest to the Steele-Dawson school district can see that writing on the wall and there are a few kids already coming to Steele.

The reason for the demise of a lot of these small town schools is not that there are fewer town kids. Farm kids were always the backbone of the schools. Large farm families were very common because rightly or wrongly, kids served as a labor pool on the early farms. That was especially true during the homesteading period and so the balance leaned even more toward the farm kids during those years. Most homesteading was done about 10 to 15 years either side of the beginning of the 20th century. A typical section (square mile) of land had from two to as many as four homesteads on it. A homestead was normally 160 acres or a quarter of a section. If you wanted another 160 acres you could make a tree claim. In order to do that you had to plant a few acres of trees and keep them alive. You could get a third quarter section too under the Homestead Act, but it was pretty much a purchase, albeit at bargain pricing. That was pretty rare, not many homesteaders had that much extra cash. So the most farms possible on a section was four and at the least there were usually two.

So let's do a little ciphering to see if we can get an idea of about how many homesteaders kids were in a township. In a township there are 36 sections. The earliest townships that were settled were along railroads. If the township was along a railroad, the railroad owned every other section, so they were not available to be homesteaded. They were for sale and because a homestead was pretty much free to the person who developed it, the railroad sections were almost always settled later. So a typical township had 18 sections that could be homesteaded on, and we've already said each section probably had from two to four farms on it. Let's say that on average there were about 2.5 farms per section. That meant a typical township probably had in the neighborhood of 45 farms in it. 45 is actually a very conservative number. Historical records show that Clear Lake Township, when my Great Grandfather Henry homesteaded there, had 58 farms and also 2 schools. Let's also assume that 20 of the farmsteads had a couple of childbearing age on it. One more assumption that we'll make is that each of the 20 had, on average, three kids. That meant there may have been as many as 60 or more kids in a typical township.

That same township today may have a dozen farms on all 36 of its sections and may only have, let's say 3 couples of childbearing age and that may be high. They would typically have about 2 kids each for a total of 6 in the township. Now that's a huge difference 60 versus 6. That's the way it is in rural areas today, farm numbers are down, average farm size is way up, the average age of the farmers is up and the numbers of children on the farms are way down.

The population of Steele has remained surprisingly stable over the years. I'm sure the population today is a little bit older on the average than it was in the 20th century. The population has never risen much over 800 and has never dropped below 600. In the 2000 Federal Census they counted 761 residents. In 2004 it was estimated to be 714. Over the last 45 years the population of Kidder County has dropped more than 50%. The 1960 census counted 5386 citizens, while the 2005 estimate was 2481, a drop of some 54%. Over that same period Steele only dropped from about 800 to 714. Currently the 8 county towns have a total of 1241 residents. The county population is split almost exactly between town and rural. The 1240 rural residents live on 584 farms, so there are only 2.1 people per farm. Noting those numbers, it is easy to see why the county schools and businesses have been decimated. Those numbers coincide with large increases in the most populous counties, particularly in Burleigh and Cass counties, where Bismarck and Fargo are located respectively.

So the stage is set for the possible final chapter for Steele and Kidder County. Will the Buffalo Commons come to central North Dakota? Steele has survived for 125 years, how much longer will it survive? With the newest computer technology there is a very good chance that work at home employees will become more common, and towns like Steele may benefit greatly from it. The newest technology will make it easier for large data input and billing companies to disperse a little and instead of people driving to Bismarck, they could possibly gather or work at home in Steele.

Steele has seen quite a bit of change since I was a kid. When I was little, it had the Bank of Steele. There were Texaco, Standard and Skelly gas stations. Probably the most incredible thing was that there were Ford, General Motors, Studebaker, and Chrysler dealerships in Steele. How, on God's green earth, did a town of 800 people support four auto dealerships? We had Allis Chalmers, John Deere and IH farm implement dealers (actually there was another, you could also buy Ford farm equipment at the Ford dealership). There was Lindy's jewelry store, Yanken and Mullen drug stores, Northside and Tollefson's and later Grosz Brothers grocery stores. There was Albright's hardware store, the Federated clothing store, Ness' variety store, the Roxy movie theater (eventually replaced by the Crown Lanes bowling alley), and the OK Motel. There were the Cave, Corner, and Nona's bars and an optometrist, JJ Hochhalter. There was Jake's and then Ray's barber shop, The Beauty Hut beauty parlor and, as we said, a doctor, Dr. Zukowsky and a dentist, Doc Needham. There was Barta's Lumberyard and also a public livestock weighing and shipping facility. At one time there were as many as three active grain elevators. It was very much a self-contained community. Many citizens of Steele rarely if ever left town. There was no need to; everything they had to have was there.

However, storm clouds were building, because what was called the interstate highway system was already in the planning stages. The intent of the interstate highway system was that in times of emergency or war, the country would have a "hard" network of roads to move troops, tanks and other heavy materials easily around the country.

Although Steele people always had good access to Highway 10 (the major east-west state highway before I-94) and it went right by Steele, it seemed like it was used only if it had to be. But building the interstate highway changed the face of Steele forever. The interstate highway system in America started a whole new traveling mentality. Before it was built, people always said "We can't go there, it's a hundred miles away". That attitude changed to, "Let's go, it's only a hundred miles away". When the access road to the interstate on-off ramps was built through the north side of Steele, it was like waving the green flag at a Nextel cup event; the race was on. You wouldn't think that a single short road would make that much difference, but it was like taking the lid off a honey jar. It seemed to attract drivers, like ants are attracted to the sweetness. The conservative travel plans of the denizens of Steele were suddenly changed, replaced by a "gas up and let's go" philosophy. The death knell of Steele as a self-contained town had sounded. That's just a layman's view but I think it's pretty accurate. One other thing to consider was that pretty much coinciding with the building of the interstate, cars and tires were seeing marked improvements, so people could more safely travel the 80 miles back and forth from Bismarck or the 120 miles back and forth from Jamestown. Cars and tires had to be better; the new interstate speed limits were 75 mph!

The gas station and truck stop built out by the highway also attracted a lot of traffic, but they were built many years after the interstate went through. Just the presence of the interstate highway itself changed Steele forever in my eyes. As I recall the east-west interstate (I-94) in North Dakota was completed in the Steele area in the mid 1960's.

While it was being built in the Steele area, over one weekend when no one was working, my cousin and I were wandering around looking over the project, just north of Steele. They had just finished the over pass bridge so we could cross it. We were on bikes, just across the bridge, north of town. We were looking down the slope on the east side of the north approach to the bridge. I don't remember who thought of this first, but we decided it would be fun to ride our bikes down this slope, which was about 150-200 feet at about a 35-40-degree angle. So off we go down the slope. We got about half way down and we see there is about a foot high ridge that a maintainer had made across the bottom. I think we both hollered "oh, no" at the same time and shortly after we hollered, both of us were launched into the air. Mercifully, we separated from our bikes and with a cloud of dust completed the ride in a heap, in the dirt. You know, neither one of us suggested we try it again.

So, as cars and highways got better, my hometown slowly lost its self contained status as business after business closed, finding they couldn't compete with their larger versions in Bismarck and Jamestown. It took quite a few years, but it slowly turned into more of a bedroom community. The only remaining original businesses are a couple of the bars, the bank, a drug store, a gas station and a grocery store. You can still get your milk and bread, your booze, your prescriptions filled, and of course, your religious needs filled. Beyond that, you're out of luck. Small town businesses find it impossible to compete with the bigger towns and their Walmarts, Kmarts, Targets, high volume car dealerships and grocery supermarkets. There has been a motel and restaurant built out by the highway and the lone remaining gas station has been expanded to include a convenience store and truckstop. Standing tall alongside the motel is Steele's own, Sandy, the World's Largest Sandhill Crane.

I should give you a little background as to why the World's Largest Sandhill Crane resides in Steele. The Steele area has long been one of the sandhill crane's major fall migration stops. Historically, the Long Lake National Wildlife Refuge south of town and the Alkali Flats southeast of town host some very large numbers of sandhill cranes when they pause during their southward migration in the fall.

One thing that Steele still has that most small towns don't have is a number of good jobs. You don't have to be stuck selling coffee and deep fried doughnuts at the convenience store. There are several potential employers. One of them is the SEI call center that services fast food vendors countrywide. Northland Financial (formerly the Bank of Steele, an all-purpose financial institution, to manage your money, invest, sell insurance) with branches in Bismarck and I think it still has one in Medina. BEK Telecommunications company (a rural phone co-op, they took over quite a bit of US West territory when they pulled out of rural areas) is probably the town's largest employer. Also, there is the school district, the nursing home and the county government. Like we said a little earlier, Steele turned 125 this year (2006)! Happy Birthday!

CHAPTER 3

NORTH DAKOTA- PEOPLE AND THINGS

When Gail and I were first married, we lived in Garrison, 75 miles north of Bismarck in central North Dakota. There we met and got to know some pretty remarkable people. North Dakota has lots of innovative, self-reliant people like John Chickosky. He was one of the maintenance men at the local hospital at Garrison. John is one of those guys who can do almost anything, whether it involves electrical work, plumbing, computers, ditch digging or rocket science. Not only is John talented, he is also one of the nicest people I've ever known. I hadn't spent much time ice fishing before I met him. He is probably the single greatest reason ice fishing became so important to me. He invited me along ice fishing and allowed us to use his fish house when he wasn't using it. As if that wasn't enough, he actually gave me an old power ice auger. He was married, his first and only marriage, to a widow, Florence, when he was in his fifties. As the great Forrest Gump once said, "they were like peas and carrots". They are probably the most compatible pair I've ever known. John and Florence allowed Gail and me and some friends of ours to build our own fish house on the farmstead that the two of them lived on. Florence rarely, if ever, missed a chance to go ice fishing with John. A nephew of theirs was a pretty good artist and he painted scenes of Snoopy (the Charlie Brown character) on their fish house. It really stood out in a crowd and was a real conversation piece. It was, without a doubt, the most photographed fish house in central North Dakota.

In North Dakota, for some reason, people with talents like John's are quite common, but I have no point of reference to conclude that there are more or less of them here than in other parts of the country. However, I was very fortunate to work with another guy, my partner Bob, who has similar abilities, for almost 25 years. You would have thought a little of that would have rubbed off on me over the years, but my wife still doesn't trust me with power tools.

As a good example of just how small a state, population wise, we live in, John's wife, Florence has two kids, a daughter Joyce and I think John is her son's name. I met both of them when I was going to college in Fargo long before I knew their mother.

Another extra-ordinary person in Garrison was a Catholic nun and laboratory technician, Sister Moira Paulus. She worked for me when I ran the lab at the hospital. She was a vintner of great ability, just what you would expect from a Catholic Benedictine nun. She was so good that locals used to bring her batches of wine that weren't turning out right and she would fix them. She used to give Gail and me wine as a Christmas present, always something different and always good.

That brings us to the most remarkable person we knew during our Garrison days. That person was the consummate small town doctor, Dr. John Boyle. If you were a recent graduate of Holy Cross University in Massachusetts who had completed a residency and had the world at your feet, where would you go to practice? Isn't the answer obvious, you'd head out into the wilds of North Dakota and never look back. That was Dr. Boyle back around 1950. He was probably the most beloved person in Garrison. He spent his entire career in Garrison and eventually died there. He would come up to the lab every day, supposedly to check his patient's lab results, but it was mostly just to visit. He delivered one of our kids and would have delivered both but was out of town when Gail went into labor. The doctor covering for him panicked and sent us to Bismarck to deliver our first baby. I wonder if Dr. Boyle ever regretted spending his life out here, wishing he'd gone back east? I guess we'll never know.

While living in Garrison we were friends with a nice couple, Marlan, an employee of the local newspaper, and his wife Nancy. Our kids were pretty close together in age even though Marlan was more than 10 years older than I was. Marlan loved sports and the outdoors, particularly fishing.

Marlan and I fished together quite often. Now as hard as Marlan tried to just live a normal life, the gods just wouldn't allow him to. It seemed like something was always out of kilter in Marlan's life. For instance, this was how one summer fishing outing went. We had gone fishing late one afternoon. Marlan had just bought a new graphite rod (graphite rods were the newest, bestest things in those days) and that afternoon, he put it into use. We had caught a couple walleyes, nothing too big. Marlan got a bite on his new rod. He fed the fish some line, waited a few seconds, tightened up the line and set the hook. When he set the hook, the rod snapped in two. He was excited and he was saying he was sure this was a six or seven pound fish or bigger. Well when he got it in and I netted it, it was a sauger that may have weighed a pound and a half. Then Marlan started cussing the store he bought it from. I wasn't listening. I was laughing too hard.

All of this happened just after we (in Marlan's boat) had to be towed back to the boat ramp. His recently repaired boat motor didn't stay repaired for very long. The key that keeps the flywheel from turning on the crankshaft sheared off when we were attempting to start the motor, which of course, left us stranded two or threes miles from the boat ramp. You see what he was up against?

Marlan is the only guy I've ever seen hook a seagull right in mid air while casting a crank bait. That was an adventure! Let me tell you right now, there is no reasoning with a seagull. A seagull's beak doesn't look like it could inflict pain, but take it from me, it is a weapon!

On the scary side, Marlan is also the only person I know who has sunk a fishing boat. It was an older craft, built before 1970, so it probably didn't have all the safety features. He and his passenger were lucky, they were close to the Highway 83 embankment and they got to the rocks in just a couple minutes. Another boat was nearby and picked them up from the rocks and took them to the boat ramp.

The first fishing boat I had was a shared one between Marlan and I. It was a 14-foot Lund with a 25-horse motor on it.

Currently, one of the most popular outdoor magazines in North Dakota is a magazine called Dakota Country. Marlan started editing that publication over 25 years ago with a little (very little) help from me. We talked about it and collected ideas for a couple years. The publisher sold the magazine to its current owner after a year or two. The rest is history. It's too bad that Marlan couldn't have stayed involved in the magazine, but he couldn't afford to foot the publishing bill until the magazine was successful enough to fly on its own. He would have loved to have kept it.

Rick was another employee of the newspaper that I met through Marlan. Rick was a real outdoorsy guy. He left the paper before we left Garrison and moved his family out to northwest Montana, I think either to the Whitefish or Kalispell area. One day he had his family out camping along a trail way up in the mountains. The sky gradually darkened during mid-day and a fine dust started dropping from the sky. Of course, they were out of commercial radio range, so they couldn't find out what was going on. They were frightened and worried so they picked up their camp and headed down the mountain.

Rick had himself thoroughly convinced that a nuclear war had started. It wasn't until the got back in AM radio range that they learned it wasn't a nuclear attack, but that Mt. St. Helens in Washington had blown up. That would have spooked just about anyone!

Who could forget these spellbinding words "When North Dakota parents send their children out to play, they fill their pockets full of rocks, so they won't blow away." Now that beats Robert Frost's poetry all to heck doesn't it? Have you ever heard of a cowboy poet? North Dakota is actually quite famous for its cowboy poets. They'll never be confused with Walt Whitman or T.S. Eliot, but they certainly are much more entertaining to a country boy like me. Credit for writing that verse goes to a gentleman by the name of Rodney Nelson, a rancher and cowboy poet in western North Dakota. You'll never confuse a cowboy poet with an inner-city rapper just by looking at them, but to be very honest, there are some similarities in their products. The rhythm and story telling are not all that different, if you are reading it. If you are listening to it being read or sung, I will have to admit that the speed of their deliveries is completely different. No one speaks slower than a cowboy does. Of course, cowboy poets also talk or write about things that are more associated with home and hearth, while rappers talk about drug dealers and killing cops. Very rarely do rappers talk about the mare dropping a foal, kids, or the weather.

As you drive around North Dakota you can't help but notice that North Dakotans seem to be fond of large fiberglass and concrete animal statues. The reasons aren't entirely clear, but there are plenty of big animal reproductions. On a per capita basis, there is probably a higher concentration here than anywhere else. If you enter the state from the west on I-94, you can't help but notice the giant black and white Holstein cow, Salem Sue, at New Salem, about 30 miles west of Bismarck. It puts Bemidji, Minnesota's Paul Bunyan and Babe the Blue Ox to shame. If you drive another 70 miles east, Steele proudly displays Sandy, the World's Largest Sandhill Crane. Driving another 60 miles east will get you to Jamestown where you'll see the biggest buffalo you've ever seen, along with an honest to goodness, live, white buffalo, White Cloud. If you continue searching, you'll find the huge Willy the Walleye north of Bismarck, in Garrison and giant turtles at Dunseith and at the aptly named Turtle Lake. Bottineau has Tommy the Turtle on a snowmobile up at the edge of the Turtle Mountains. There is a huge catfish out in Wahpeton, in the Red River valley, and a whole array of large metal animals, including pheasants, geese, grasshoppers and deer along the Enchanted Highway in southwest North Dakota.

The Enchanted Highway is mostly the work of one person; a man named Gary Greff. The highway is a 32-mile stretch of road from I-94's exit 72 south to the little town of Regent. It currently has six groups of metal sculptures that include the Tin Family (they look like the Wizard of Oz' tin man), a flock of geese, a pheasant family, grasshoppers, some deer and a scene that features Teddy Roosevelt. Mr. Greff is adding a fishing scene soon and has plans for other sculptures also.

My family's farm is just across the interstate from Steele on the northeast corner of the Steele interchange. There is a picture window in front of the house where the living room is located that looks out on the interstate highway, not much more than 100 yards away.

One day, my youngest brother was sitting in the living room watching television and couldn't help but notice several law enforcement vehicles coming down the off ramp. Among the vehicles was that of a county sheriff's deputy and one belonging to a highway patrolman. They set up a roadblock and were stopping all westbound vehicles.

We found out later, the reason they had blocked the road was to stop a car that had fled from police in Jamestown (60 miles east). The law enforcement people had been told the occupants of that car were believed to be armed and the vehicle they were driving was reported to be stolen. I know the people in the car weren't from North Dakota, but I don't remember what they did to get in such a pickle. Anyway, all the activity piqued Darin's interest. To get a better look at what was going on, Darin went out in the front yard and Dad joined him. They were standing in the yard a couple minutes later when the car the police were looking for drove up. The highway was completely blocked. The patrolman and the deputy, guns in their hands, approached the vehicle from both sides. Suddenly a shot rang out from inside the car with the bullet striking the deputy in the face, injuring him. At that point the state trooper didn't hesitate, he rushed the car and put two or three rounds from his shotgun into the backseat of the car, where the shot had come from, and if I remember right, he killed one and wounded another of the occupants. State law says that if there is a death as the result of criminal activity no matter what or who caused the death, the offenders are charged with murder, so the occupants of the car were in deep doo-doo.

Now that's something you don't see every day, a shootout right out of your front yard! The bad thing was that Darin and Dad had no idea what was going on. A more experienced police officer would have either evacuated the house or at the very least stopped and told them what was going on and asked whoever was home to stay under cover. That's a problem caused by too little crime. In all the years since then, I don't remember anything else similar to that anywhere in the state.

While we're talking about crime sprees, let's talk about bank holdups, after all this is practically the wild west. For a few years, the State Bank of Burleigh County had a small branch bank at Sterling, right at the intersection of I-94 and US Highway 83, about 22 miles east of Bismarck. They had moved it out to the interstate from the original town site at least a mile to the south. (They built a new building, and moved the business, they didn't move the old bank.)

Sterling is a tiny town population wise, but is spread out over quite a large area. The town has gradually spread north following the construction of, first, Highway 10 and then I-94. There are no local police. It seemed like every time a criminal type was passing through the state they recognized the fairly easy escape possibilities along with the bank's relative isolation, and they robbed that bank. The teller, a nice, harmless, middle aged woman, was pistol-whipped during one of the robberies. A Highway patrolman was shot (not fatally) during another one of the hold-ups. Although the bank building was just built in 1982, the branch was closed many years ago, probably because of the buildings suspect location. During the time it was open, it was robbed those two times and it seems like there was a third time, probably the only bank holdups in the entire state during that time period.

We can't forget to mention something that helps make North Dakota so special. A lot of us probably already know the answer to this question. What fruit makes the best jelly and pancake syrup in the world? Here's a hint; it's not strawberries, raspberries, peaches, blueberries or juneberries. Yeah, you got it. It's chokecherries (of course). Some of you may not know what chokecherries are. I know they aren't just present on the northern plains, but I think they're most commonly used here. We had a big patch of chokecherries in our yard and the fruit was a staple of our diet in late summer.

So, just what are chokecherries? The bushes they grow on are actually small trees that in the spring are covered with bunches of white blossoms. The fruit develops in bunches also. Chokecherries, when ripe, are a small deep purple round fruit with a pit in the middle. There is so little pulp with the fruit that we used to fill our mouths with berries and work off the skin and pulp, then spit out the pits like a machine gun.

You could always tell when a kid had been eating chokecherries because his teeth were purple.

If you were a grouse hunter, you quickly learned that fermented chokecherries are the bird's favorite food. Knowing that, you moved from chokecherry patch to chokecherry patch. You always found them (you're really looking for the tipsy ones, from eating the fermented berries).

At our house there was an event that took place every summer toward the end of August. One morning we would get up, go downstairs, and on the kitchen table there would a half dozen buckets of all sizes. It was chokecherry picking day! Knowing what we would get in return, we all pitched in and filled them with ripe berries.

Growing up on the plains certainly had its drawbacks. We were a million miles from anywhere (Have you ever been to Grenora, ND? It's even a little bit further). We are on the leading edge of nothing except raising spring wheat, flax and sunflowers. To those of you that don't know what a sunflower is, it's not just the pretty little yellow flower that grows wild. Not exactly. It's a beefed up hybrid of that wild flower that is raised for it's seeds, either to roast and eat or to be crushed for "Sun Oil". You've eaten sunflower seeds I'm sure. Edible sunflowers are referred to as confectionery sunflowers. Those that are crushed for oil are called, strangely enough, oil sunflowers. We lead the nation in the production of both confectionery and oil sunflowers.

But, leading the nation in sunflower production doesn't get you on the cover of Time magazine. There were very few wealthy people in the state, especially in small towns. There wasn't a rock singer that had sold a million records anywhere in sight. What I am trying to say is that none of us lived in the lap of luxury and/or had access to the finer things in life and/or was famous. In spite of that, and in spite of living 40 miles via interstate highway from North Dakota's capital and second largest city, we thought that for small town kids, we were pretty much out on the leading edge of most of the new music, clothing, and sports trends. We definitely didn't have an inferiority complex. The truth was we had no idea what it was like in the real world, something we were, in reality, content to leave undiscovered. That's the beauty of living here in the northern Great Plains, to a certain extent there was no reason that anything that was going on out on the coasts should matter to us. In effect, we got to pick and choose what things we wanted to be a part of our lives. 1500 miles makes a great buffer zone, and because of that, we did not participate, among other things, in the whole drug scene of the bigger cities and the anti-war rallies of the late 60's.

The German-Russian triangle was an area of thousands of square miles mostly to the south of us that was heavily homesteaded by, yeah, you got it, Germans from Russia. Bandleader Lawrence Welk, another well-known North Dakotan and Teddy Roosevelt Roughrider Award winner, was from that area. When the ancestors of these people left Germany for Russia some time ago, they pledged to keep their native language and to not let their culture be influenced by other local cultures. Because of that they did not attend local schools and of course spoke German at home. They continued that policy in America. World War I opened their eyes somewhat, when they had to deal with locals who mistrusted them and considered them enemies because of their policies of staying so ethnic. At that time, they became more amenable to changes. Because the German-Russians were so concentrated in some areas, sometimes the changes came quite slowly.

We always had a notion that we were much more modern than the kids behind the "Sauerkraut Wall" in the German-Russian triangle were. When we played high school basketball in one of the towns (in what is probably the most concentrated German-Russian area in south central North Dakota) in about 1968, the hometown cheerleaders cheered with a German brogue. It would be rude to say it was comical, but it was very interesting, to say the least, when those high schoolgirls cheered "Yump, Yump sky high, tip it to a Lehr guy". We always considered them to be a little bit behind times, that they were, as we used to say, "right off the farm." They probably had their own ideas about us. I'd bet money that they disagreed with our assessment of them as much as we disagreed with their assessment of us. Even after all the years there was still a little mistrust and lack of knowledge about each other.

We would reason because our basketball team wore low top athletic shoes before any one else, or because we had the latest Stones or Beatles album, or because we dated big city Bismarck girls, or because we had seen the latest James Bond movie, that these things made us more cosmopolitan than the German-Russian kids were. We thought we were, as they used to say in the 60's and 70's, pretty "cool". 'Thought' is the key word here. What we didn't know was that cool wasn't something you wore or something you earned because you did all the sociably acceptable things. You want to know what real cool is? In my mind, it was much simpler than we made it out to be, but requires a little thought and giving of yourself. As they say, "actions speak louder than words". Real cool was your father working extra hours to send you to that football camp you wanted to go to, or your mother working far into the night to alter that jacket you wanted to wear to the Spring Dance. You don't wear cool on your sleeve, you live it.

For those of you that don't know much about the reasons there were German–Russians, I'll give a little background. When Catherine the Great was the Czarina of Russia, she recognized that Russia had huge tracts of land in the Lower Volga River area that were suitable for agriculture, but there were no farmers in Russia to fill that void. So in the late 1700's the Russian government advertised in Germany for farmers to relocate to that area. In return, for populating and developing the lands along the lower Volga, they would get the farmland at a low cost and the youth of the Germans would not have to serve in the military, on a perpetual basis. A lot of Germans answered the call. After quite some time, the rulers of Russia started to ignore their promises and in 1874 started to force the German youth to serve in the military. That spurred a huge immigration of the Germans out of Russia and to America. That's the short version of the story of the German-Russians.

The next question begging to be asked is why did the German-Russians so heavily populate central North and South Dakota. (They settled in large numbers in north central South Dakota also.) The answer to that question I have found is really quite simple. The areas where they settled most strongly reminded them of the areas of Russia they had just left.

The German-Russian triangle encompasses a large part of North Dakota. Get your map out and follow along. It extends from Bowman in the southwest corner, up through Dickinson, northeast to Rugby and south from there to about Ellendale on the South Dakota border. People of German-Russian descent comprise nearly half (48%) of North Dakota's current population.

Steele is almost in the middle of the German-Russian triangle, and while we have our share of people of German-Russian heritage, Steele has a much more diverse population. I think it was that way because Steele is right on the Northern Pacific main line. You just never knew who was going to drop in for supper. It's population also includes Scandinavians, quite a few people of English, Scotch, and Welsh descent, and some Germans from Germany (Reichsdeutsch) and originally, as we talked about earlier, a few black families.

Elsewhere in North Dakota, Norwegians settled in the eastern part of North Dakota, up and down the entire length of the Red River valley. Scandinavians also settled along the Canadian border and they included Swedes and Danes as well as Norwegians. There were Icelanders that came to North

Dakota and they settled mostly in the Pembina area, in the northeast corner of the state. People that are of Norwegian descent make up about a third (31%) of the state's population, with much smaller percentages (less than 5% each) descended from Swedes, Danes and Icelanders. So nearly 80 % of North Dakotans are descended from either German-Russian or Norwegian ancestors.

Do you believe in fate? An elderly Norwegian farmer once told me his ancestors, the Vikings (not the Minnesota Vikings) believed that their lives were preordained. They believed that the time and place of their death was already pre-determined, and nothing they did in their life would change that. Because their fate was already sealed, it didn't matter what risks they took or didn't take in battle; they were going to die when their time came. They would fight like maniacs (or as we would say today, go berserk), because they didn't fear death. I've discovered that the word "berserk" originated in Norway. It origin was as the name of a group of fearless Viking warriors, the "berserkers", the world's original "shock" troops. Learning never ends.

Although most North Dakotans would deny it, there is a Northern Plains dialect of the English language. The Norwegians contributed "Uff-da" and "Yeah you betcha" to the northern plains dialect. The German-Russians also contributed to the local dialect, with their pronunciation of some words, (like paggitch instead of package) and their peculiar habit of butchering sentence structure, i.e. "It rained last night and the water is running over the road still" or "The cow, she jumped over the fence". North Dakotans call bottled or canned soda, "pop", they call the sofa, a "couch", they call a casserole, a "hot dish". They will end a sentence or conversation with "ya know", "you betcha", or "okie dokie". They also tend to end sentences with a preposition, like "Do you want to come with"? It's not exactly a foreign language; it just seems like it.

In many small towns, especially those in what would be considered the most isolated areas of the state, it's sad to report, but there is a greater than normal incidence of alcoholism. The causes are varied, but most times it is boredom. They needed to find things to do. Most small towns, including Steele, had at least a few chronic alcoholics. Some people just never find anything else to do except to go down to the local watering hole and spend their evenings there.

In our town when I was growing up, one of the most visible of those alcoholics was an old railroad man, Hjalmer. When he left the bar and worked his way home to the north up Mitchell Avenue (Steele's main north-south street), he had animated discussions with every sign post and power pole from the Corner Bar to his house. Sometimes he just spoke to nothing. We were all used to it. Hjalmer was a fixture in Steele. Of course, he wasn't the only one with a drinking problem. There were also one or two old alcoholics that drove to the bar. An old bachelor farmer nicknamed Shorty was one of these. The local policeman would keep an eye out for them leaving the bar and they would get a police escort home or in Shorty's case out of town at about 5 miles an hour. Shorty lived in a rural area just three or four miles out of town. Only in a small town would you get treatment like that. I would think many small towns had similar characters.

Another thing you used to see at the small town bars, always just on weekends, were the family cars of the Saturday night, out on the town drinkers. They were lined up outside the bar and at least a couple of them, sometimes more, had kids in the backseat. In Steele going to the bar and socializing was one of the main forms of weekend recreation. Although it seems there should have been somewhere else to socialize, where would that be? The kids in the cars were almost always farm kids whose folks couldn't find babysitters in their rural area. They visited and played games with each other and when they got tired, they would curl up in a blanket and go to sleep. For the kids it wasn't just part of growing up; it was their Saturday night socializing too.

In most small North Dakota towns, the first daily order of business for a loosely associated group of men, the men's morning coffee bunch is to gather for their morning cup of coffee. Steele is no exception. The group historically has gathered in what used to be the bowling alley and café and is now just a café. I'm not sure the café at the bowling alley is still open. That would leave the Coffee Cup (the gas station) as the next most likely place to meet. I'm sure they're still active, it's just a matter of where. They sit and drink their coffee and, of course, talk for an hour or better, going through the latest rumors floating around town. Although they would never admit it, they are the towns unofficial town gossip society. They don't really solve any problems. That's probably beyond their powers, and no one really expects them to solve anything. I would bet you that one of the things they occasionally talk about is how much some of the older ladies in town spread gossip. They are an integral part of any small community, the men's morning coffee bunch.

We had an optometrist in Steele, when I was a kid, who was a fairly elderly man named J.J. Hochhalter. To us kids he was an interesting old fellow. He used to build miniature fully operational, steam engines. Now there's nothing more interesting to a kid than the unknown. Because I didn't own a copy of "The Kid's Pocket Guide to Physics", we only had a vague idea as to how his engines worked. They were fascinating. After watching him run one a few times we pretty much caught on. We were able to deduce a lot about engines in general once we understood a little bit about the power of compressed gases.

In the 1963-64 school year I was in the sixth grade and had turned 11 years old. Two monumental things happened that year. On Nov. 22nd, 1963 a man named Lee Harvey Oswald shot and killed President Kennedy during the president's visit to

Dallas, Texas. That was a very dark day in my life. I was just old enough to realize what a great man President Kennedy was and what a loss to the country his death would be. President Kennedy's assassination exposed us to the stark reality of his death, and so cheated us out of a little bit of our childhood and a lot of our innocence. School was dismissed until the president was buried. Of course the entire proceedings were televised. My sister and I were glued to the TV set. It was history in the making, very sad history, but nonetheless history. The second event occurred on Feb. 9th, 1964, when the Beatles appeared on the Ed Sullivan Show. That night heralded the beginning of what was called the British Invasion. I don't know what it was about the Beatles that was so attractive to me. It's not like they were great musicians; they were better showmen than musicians. That night, watching Ed Sullivan, I suddenly realized that music was a lot of fun. Before that night I had never really paid attention to it. After that night there was always a song playing in my head. My life was changed forever by those two events and both happened to take place during my sixth grade year, an extraordinary year in a very ordinary life.

When we were eighth graders, the hormones were just starting to flow through us boys. We had a teacher that year whose first name I don't remember. I just remember her last name, Miss Vossler. She wasn't in our room all the time but quite often. She was quite attractive, and that was at a time when most of us boys were beginning to notice things like that. One day, one of my classmates, Doug, was out of the room for a few minutes. Miss Vossler left her desk and sat in one of the student desks while he was gone. Doug came back in the room and when he did, he didn't see Miss Vossler at her desk in front of the room. He apparently didn't look around too much. He stood in front of the room and said in a provocative voice, "Where's Hossy Vossy"? Miss Vossler didn't say a word and just raised her hand. Then Doug saw her and turned about seventeen different shades of red.

When you were in school, did you have a teacher that was such a good teacher that you really looked forward to go to his or her class? Maybe you had several. On the other hand were there any teachers that you always felt you weren't getting your parent's tax dollars worth with? Just what makes a good teacher? It seemed that the best teachers were truly interested in the subject they taught, and because of their enthusiasm, they always made learning easy and fun. The best teachers also really liked their students and made it part of their job to learn more about them. The poorer teachers just went through the motions; it was just a job to them. You really can't fool the kids. If the teacher isn't interested in teaching, they aren't interested in learning. Those teachers were cannon fodder for some of the meaner kids. That teacher's method of coping with the student's lack of interest and poor behavior was a steady stream of students out of their classroom to visit the principal. They were always sparring with their kids. Our high school principal was one of my favorites. He did kick me out of school once, but I did deserve it. As they say, if you play you pay. He was always caught between the students and the teacher. I didn't envy him. However he did recognize that not all things were the fault of the student and he wasn't afraid to tell us that. He was always honest with us and we appreciated it.

I thought the best teacher I had in high school was my high school music teacher. He was also the most demanding. If you weren't into music, you probably didn't like him. He drove you pretty hard. He did one thing that I would have never thought possible. In my junior year, he talked me into taking the part of Colonel Pickering (one of the two male leads, the other was Henry Higgens) in the musical "My Fair Lady". That production was probably the single most enjoyable thing I did in high school. If you would have asked me before we did the musical if there was any way on in the world that I would enjoy something like that, I would have laughed at you for asking such a silly question.

I'll never forget, a year and a half later, during my freshman year in college, the movie version of "My Fair Lady", with Rex Harrison, Audrey Hepburn and Wilfrid Hyde-White, was playing in a Fargo theater. I asked all of my buddies if they would like to see it with me and they all said, "are you kidding me"? I went alone. I couldn't even get a date to go along with me.

The young lady that played the part of the "My Fair Lady" female lead, Eliza Doolittle, was Marlys, who was a year ahead of me in high school. She was a very pretty and talented girl. Marlys was a young lady that always made you feel like you were special. She would grab your arm, call you "Dear", and sometimes lay her head on your shoulder. I've had similar experiences with other girls, but the thing that separated Marlys from those other girls was that she was sincere. You knew she wasn't just jerking you around. In fact, after our final performance of our musical, which incidentally was staged during a snowstorm, without electrical power, Marlys grabbed me and laid an unforgettable kiss on me. It was practically the highlight of my junior year in high school! Today she is still a remarkably good-looking lady, and I know she's about my age but unless you knew that, you would have a hard time guessing her age. You'll read a little bit about her dad, Vic, a little later. He was also a good friend of ours in our younger days.

That final performance without power was quite an experience. The show must go on, as they say in the business. And it did, even though we did it by flashlight and without an orchestra. That was also unforgettable!

In general we had very good teachers in Steele, but when I was going to high school, we didn't have particularly good coaches. You do have to keep things in perspective though. We weren't in school to learn how to play any particular sport.

We were there to prepare ourselves for life. I understood that, but it still would have been nice to have better coaching so we could have been more than a doormat to the Emmons Centrals and Lintons (the schools with really good athletic programs in our area) that we faced. But it just wasn't to be. In small towns, it's hard to attract good coaches and harder still to retain them. If anyone complained about the coaching, our administrators would say, what's most important here? It seemed at the time, they felt just having a qualified and willing coach was good enough. They were more right than wrong.

Actually in a small school it is quite hard to consistently get good coaches. If a coach leaves and has to be replaced, you may need to find a coach that, for instance, could teach keyboarding and chemistry or some other odd combination of teaching assignments.

I only had one of what I would consider to be a very good coach while I was in high school. That was our baseball coach. We all liked him and he did a great job of preparing us. We had some good, talented baseball teams when I was in high school. We were well prepared, but we always ran into a hot pitcher or another good team and got knocked off, so we never contended for a state title.

Our football coach was fresh out of college and although he knew football and tried hard, he was so inexperienced that he didn't stand a chance against the Al Dosch's (Emmons Central's coach, a North Dakota coaching legend) of our world. When he arrived at Steele High School in my junior year he was the third different coach we had had in three years.

Our basketball coach actually was quite a good coach, but he was a poor personnel manager. He would let a couple of the kids routinely skip practice. Of course the rest of us loved that. That didn't seem to be the way to build camaraderie and a winning attitude. I actually think that if the assistant coach we had as a senior, had been the head coach, we would have had a much better team. But, that was a really long time ago. What's going on today at Steele-Dawson High.

Today, Steele-Dawson High has a couple of really good coaches, especially in the girl's programs, and in general their coaching staff is better than average. I don't know if they are trying harder to get good coaches or if they just got lucky. The end result is that they seem to be developing more of a winning attitude. Now, winning in sports isn't everything, but it certainly does make high school more fun. I personally feel that high school sports are quite important and that maybe high school is, and always will be, much more than just academics. It seems that a well coached, winning sports program serves the dual purpose of instilling discipline and developing a winning attitude in life as well as in the sport. Sports, in my opinion, are as important as other more cultural extra-curricular activities, such as music, student government and theater, among others. And I'm not playing down the importance of those other extra-curricular activities; I participated in the three I listed, as well as played several sports.

When my little brother Darin was a high school sophomore, Steele-Dawson's basketball team was the first in the 80+ year history of the school to go to the state Class B tournament as we'll talk about in an upcoming chapter. It turned out to be the first of several for the school. It's really odd, you have to learn to win big games in almost any sport as well as in life. It seems like when you finally learn to win those big games, there is no turning back; you are a "winner". That's exactly what I mean when I refer to sports as a training ground for life, to train you to become a winner. It is just one facet of a well-rounded education.

If you want to get a little more philosophical about life and winning, you really have to wonder how many cross roads there are in your life where the choice you make determines if you are to become that winner or if you go in the tank.

On the other hand if you buy into the Viking's fate theory, your life is predetermined and then the choices don't matter. I personally like to think that the choices we make do determine the direction of our life. Those choices really aren't that hard to make, but sometimes a little training and direction helps. That's exactly where parents, schools and sports come in!

If you are a female, any time you're feeling sexually harassed or downtrodden, consider this. Our old neighbors Pastor Eric and his wife Ida Belle spent some time in Kentucky's hill country. Eric was the minister in a Methodist church there. One Sunday they were invited to dinner at one of their parishioners who lived back in the hills. When it was time to eat, Ida Belle noticed that the table had way too few settings and asked about it. She was told that the 'menfolk' eat first. So she sat and waited for the 'menfolk' to eat. When they were done, it was the 'womenfolk' and kids turn to eat. She noted the food plates looked strange when she walked in to the kitchen and asked one of the ladies, "why is all the food black?" The woman replied "oh, those darn flies" and waved her hand over the food and flushed about a million flies off of the food. Ida Belle then asked where some clean plates were and was curtly rebuffed by the hostess, who told her we don't need clean plates and turned the plate at her setting over, which was repeated by the rest of the ladies and eventually Ida Belle also. The women ate off the backside of the men's dirty plates! Now things don't seem so bad, do they?

One of our neighbors, Ed, had a light blue 1965 Chevy four wheel drive pickup. It was the first four-wheel drive I had ever seen. Ed was also a big hunter. He was the only person I knew who at the time went big game hunting in another state. He took me on my first goose hunt using decoys. I think he served as something of a role model for me. Something or someone, and it may have been him, lit a fire in me that burns to this day. I've had a forty-year love affair with the outdoors, hunting and fishing.

The generation before us in North Dakota (including our parents) lived through the great Depression and the tremendous drought of the 30's, one of the most difficult times in the state and nation's history. That generation was trained by circumstances to be the most frugal generation of North Dakotans ever. A rancher south of Steele once told me that his folks were so poor that they gave him a quarter if he would skip supper. Then during the night they would steal the quarter back from him. In the morning when his quarter was missing, they wouldn't let him eat breakfast because he had lost his quarter. Do you think that he may have been exaggerated just a little bit?

All of my life, history has just fascinated me. Since one of the great stories in North Dakota history is the story of George Armstrong Custer, and it is one of my favorites, I'll give my version of the tragedy. If you already know all you want to know about Custer in North Dakota and of his demise out in a little valley in south central Montana, just skip to the end of this chapter.

George Armstrong Custer was a West Point graduate who had seen a lot of action in the Civil War. After the war was over he was assigned to command the 7th Cavalry Regiment out on the frontier at Ft. Hayes, Kansas.

In 1873 Custer and the 7th were reassigned to Fort Abraham Lincoln near Bismarck, North Dakota. He had risen in rank to Lieutenant Colonel. Although the railroad had recently reached it, Bismarck, because of its remoteness, had to be one of the least sought after postings in the army. But that's where the action was.

Today, Fort Lincoln, which is actually south of Mandan on the west side of the Missouri River, is part of North Dakota's Fort Lincoln State Park. Many of the buildings have been meticulously restored, including the house on "Officers Row" that George and Libby Custer lived in. It has been furnished and decorated exactly the same as a couple of pictures showed it was in ca. 1875. It is a very interesting place to visit.

In August of 1873 Custer and 2 companies of the 7th were assigned to guard a railroad survey crew on what was known as the Yellowstone expedition. During that expedition they were attacked by a fairly large band of Lakota warriors. That attack was turned back by the 7th Cavalry troopers. I would almost bet that when his troopers held off those Lakota warriors, the seed of invincibility was planted in Custer's mind. In less than 3 years, that seed grew large enough to kill him. In the summer of 1874, he led an expedition into the Black Hills where engineers that were accompanying the expedition found gold in a drainage with the name of French Creek. This started the Black Hills gold rush, which in affect precipitated the events that resulted in the death of Custer and his command.

In the spring of 1876, the Lakota, Cheyenne and Arapaho, disgusted with their treatment on their reservations and the invasion of their sacred Black Hills by gold seekers, left those reservations en masse. Agents at the reservations estimated that some 12,000+ hostiles had left their homes. They were gathered somewhere in the territory that would become the states of Wyoming and Montana. When it was determined that the hostiles had gathered in what is now south central Montana, plans were drawn up to force the hostiles back to their reservations.

Around 650 of Custer's command were to be part of a three pronged assault that was designed to trap the Lakota and their allies between three forces. About 200 of their 7th, including the regimental band did not go along on the Little Bighorn expedition. The band however did accompany the troopers early in their march, playing every night, returning to Fort Lincoln after a week or so. Incidentally, on June 1-2 about 2 weeks into their march, Custer's force was halted for those two days by a very freakish June snowstorm.

The 7th was part of a force under the command of General Alfred Terry that would approach the hostiles from the east. Terry led another 600 cavalry and 400 infantry. General John Gibbons was leading a force of 450 men out of Bozeman, Montana that were closing in from the west. General George Crook was to advance out of the south with his 1000+ soldiers and scouts. They were to converge on the village of the Lakota and their allies.

The plan began to unravel when the Indians attacked and halted Crook's forces at the Rosebud Creek in what is now extreme south central Montana. A short time later, when Custer's scouts found the huge village in the valley of the Little Bighorn, Custer, against the advice of his scouts, prepared to attack the village the next morning. He had been ordered by General Terry to wait for he and Gibbons. There has always been some controversy with that order. Supposedly when Custer was given the order not to attack the village alone, he answered by saying something like "No sir, I won't", which obviously can be taken two ways.

Nonetheless, on June 25th in spite of his orders, he split the 7th into four units; 129 troopers and officers under the command of Captain McDougal were left to guard the baggage train, and he began his attack with the other three units. Major Benteen was sent with 115 troopers and officers to stop the retreat of the Indians when the attack began. Captain Reno with 142 troopers and officers and 35 scouts was to attack the huge village from the east. Custer with 204 troopers and officers and 3 civilians in his command was going to strike from the north and smash the village. This whole thing was like a half dozen flies attacking a full-grown cow with the intention of having it for supper. It just wasn't going to happen. As would be expected, Reno's assault failed and Custer, not recognizing he was greatly overmatched, rode off into infamy with all 204 men of his 7th Cavalry detachment as well as the 3 civilians. Accompanying him were his brothers

Capt. Tom Custer and Boston Custer as well as Bismarck Tribune correspondent Mark Kellogg. I'm sure that Custer imagined himself as dying gallantly in battle. But the truth is no death is gallant. I'm sure when the time came; dying didn't seem gallant to Custer at all.

Reno retreated and was eventually joined by Benteen's force and the pack train. A few of the officers felt they had to go to help Custer. They tried and were quickly turned back. They retreated back to the main force, where they all spent a couple days surrounded by the Lakota and their allies and suffered very heavy casualties. Of the 425 men in the force, they suffered 103 casualties, with 51 of those killed. With the approach of General Terry's troops on the 27th the Indians left the field and their village scattered.

While it was a great victory by the Lakota warriors and their allies, it was the beginning of the end for the great horse cultures of the Great Plains. The result of the Indian victory was that the military power of the United States as a whole was focused on defeating the Lakota and their allies. They didn't stand a chance. The finest light cavalry the world had ever seen was heavily outgunned and outmanned and by 1890 the Plains Indian Wars were effectively over. The great Lakota medicine man, Sitting Bull, went from leading the Lakota tribe to its last great victory to becoming a spectacle in Buffalo Bills Wild West Show in just a few years.

Today, it's hard to believe, but we are now becoming the elders. The kids that I started school with in 1958 and graduated from high school with in 1970 all turned 54 years old or older this year. Not too long ago, I was ice fishing on Braddock Dam, south of Steele. A couple old guys walked out on the ice and were fishing near me. After a while I thought I should go over and see how those old guys are doing. Then I realized those guys were about the same age as me! I sat and thought about that for a while. Just when did old age sneak up on me and whack me with its stick? The day certainly had come that I thought never would, I had become an elder. I didn't know if I should celebrate or cry. In the end I came to grips with it and even filled out an application to join AARP. I haven't sent it in yet. We'll take it one step at a time.

CHAPTER 4

GROWING UP IN NORTH DAKOTA

One of the great lessons in life is discovering for yourself what will happen if your tongue touches super cold metal. It's something that is usually explained to us at a very young age, but in the end most of us choose to investigate it ourselves. When I was in elementary school, we had a metal flagpole out in front of the school. It was out the front door, down some steps and about 10-15 yards straight out beyond the steps. One very cold winter day, out of the blue, I decided it was time for my lesson. I went out the front door, down the steps and to the flagpole, stuck out my tongue and presto, Mom was right, my tongue was attached to the pole. It sticks very firmly and immediately. In the absence of someone merciful that will get some warm water to pour on the pole and set you free, the only other way to quickly get free is to peel the first layer of skin off your tongue, which I did. The result was a very painful, lasting lesson in one of the facts of life. Cold flagpoles and tongues don't mix. It is said that all over North Dakota there are pieces of kid's tongues on pump handles, doorknobs, flagpoles, windmill frames and a myriad of other metal objects. It's just one of those times where curiosity overcomes common sense

Most kids are natural showoffs and we were no different. We used to stage (under neighborhood big sister, Karen's, tutelage) exhibitions of gymnastics, acting and singing in Karen's mother's garage. We would post advertising bills, make tickets, round up refreshments, and drag in an eclectic collection of chairs for seating. We had a lot of fun. Our parents probably got very sick of it, but our performances were always well attended.

Our neighborhood big sister was a high school girl, Karen, who all of us boys had a crush on and all the girls wanted to be just like. As a young lady, she owned the only monkey in Steele, heck probably the only one in Kidder County (that wasn't why we boys had a crush on her, but on the other hand, which one of us wouldn't have wanted a girlfriend with a monkey?). Although she would have resisted classification, if you had to, you would probably have referred to her as a free spirit at a time when there were very few free spirits in North Dakota. Over the years she was gradually adopted by all of us kids as our "big sister". Karen fit the part very well. It was amazing, none of the dozen or so kids that made up the neighborhood gang ever mentioned her as a "big sister", but every one of us naturally were polarized to her over time. She whole-heartedly accepted the role that was thrust on her. I don't ever remember her telling one of us to go away when we would come traipsing in the house, even if her boyfriend (and future husband) Michael was there. She was always there for us if we needed help or advice with something and she always kept us up to date with the latest food crazes. Whenever I think back to those days, Karen's smiling face is one of the first images to appear. I just can't adequately describe how important an influence she was on me in my early years. Although she never left North Dakota, I failed to stay in touch with her. First, it was going away to college, then it was getting married and raising a family. The end result was that I didn't see her for many years. But then one day, there she was again. About a year before brother Rob died, I was at the nursing home visiting him and at one point I thought

I heard a familiar voice in the hall. A couple minutes later, a gray haired Karen popped into the room and gave us both a big hug, just like we were still in the neighborhood. In spite of the philosophy that says the one thing you can count on in life is that all things will change, thank goodness, not all things do change. All of us are certainly older, and look it, but we still have our big sister.

Karen's mother and father had split before I knew the family. Their household consisted of just the mother, Lois, and her three girls Mary Jo, Karen, and Janice. It was easy to see why the girls were all attractive. Their mother, Lois, is a very attractive woman. Mary Jo was the oldest daughter. She married a brother of a classmate of mine and moved to the west coast in Washington State. Mary Jo had a beautiful singing voice. Then came Karen, who was in high school. The youngest (by quite a few years) was the very pretty Janice. Janice was just a couple of years younger than I was, so when we got older, I did date her a couple times, but that didn't work. Growing up together we actually felt more like brother and sister. How could you date a girl you had shared a mud pie with? In the end, even though I grew up with Jan, the older we got the more we grew apart. Sadly she became more of a stranger than a friend. She went her way and I went mine. Our paths haven't crossed for at least 35 years.

Meanwhile, on the homefront, when mealtimes rolled around, a North Dakota kid pretty much knew what to expect. 95% of what we ate came from a garden, wheat, oats, corn, cattle or pigs. What I'm saying is if it wasn't grown in North Dakota we probably didn't eat it. Of course there were a few things we had to get that weren't local. One of the few non-local products that we used as kids was a remarkable product called Fizzies. You just dropped a tablet in water and presto, you had a soft drink!

We weren't a big breakfast family. For breakfast we ate a variety of foods, among them homemade bread topped with cream and brown sugar (one of the all-time great foods, but maybe not featured in Health Weekly), cream of wheat, oatmeal, dry cereal, or something called coco wheats. The coco wheats were actually my favorite commercially packaged breakfast food. It was chocolate flavored cream of wheat. Who doesn't like chocolate? I still like coco wheats; some things are just good. I remember making coffee the pre-percolator and pre-coffee maker way. One of us kids would make coffee for Mom and Dad on weekend mornings while they slept in a little. We would fill the old coffeepot about 2/3 full of water. Then you floated two big scoops of ground coffee on top of the water, put it on a burner and brought it to a boil. After boiling, you took it off the heat and tossed in a little cold water. The cold water helped settle out the grounds. Then it was ready.

We had hot dogs, hamburgers and sandwiches with garden fruits and vegetables for dinner. The garden stuff made its appearance as homemade tomato or vegetable soup on cold winter days. "Exotic foods", like french fries and pizza (they were exotic to us), were just beginning to make their appearance. Karen fed me my first pizza at the age of about 8 or 9 and started a life long love affair with it. It was made with a kit you bought at the grocery store. The kit had a crust mix that you just added water to, a little can of pizza sauce and some shredded mozzarella cheese. I liked hot dogs a lot until someone told us what they were made of. Since then my brothers and I call them L & A. You can use your imagination to figure that one out. Of course, hamburger (beef) is a large part of the North Dakota farm economy and we did our best to keep it that way. The sandwiches were usually something called "minced ham" or sometimes my favorite, braunschweiger.

Suppertime was usually more varied, but always included meat and potatoes in one form or another. The meat often times was something we hunted or had caught out of a lake or river. It could have been wild duck, pheasant, or northern pike as well as chicken, beef or pork. Supper was the meal where we always sat down and ate together as a family. It wasn't in front of a TV. There was only one TV in the house and that was in the living room. Leave it to American ingenuity to overcome that little problem with TV dinners, TV trays and also portable TVs. Also, no matter how hard I tried to hide them, I always had to eat all of my peas. I hated peas. It wasn't fair, Dad refused to eat corn (he said it was pig food) and got away with it. Who says being a Dad doesn't have perks? A personal favorite of us kids was what we called hot dish. Hot dish was a concoction of hamburger, stewed tomatoes and macaroni.

Cheese Whiz and Tang were the hot new things when I was a kid. Soft spreadable cheese; what an idea! Of course Tang was known as the "space age" drink. There was also that gift from France and J. R. Simplot that was introduced to the American public in the 50's, the frozen french fry. This bringing of french fries to the masses either from the home freezer or from a fast food vendor may have been responsible for more heart disease than any other food craze. It was a little later, in my high school days, when a guy named John out in Wyoming introduced us to what has become a staple of the American diet, the taco. By the way, does anyone know happened to our Fizzies?

I grew up with several ethnic foods in my diet. I don't consider tacos, burritos or pizza ethnic foods any longer because by the time I was a teenager they were about as American as apple pie and pickled eggs. Although I'm more German (my ancestors were Reichsdeutsch or Germans from Germany, one of the **real** minorities in North Dakota, there are very few of us) than Norwegian, my favorite ethnic foods are Norwegian. The first ethnic food on my list is lefse. Lefse looks like a tortilla, but instead of making it with corn flour, it is made from mashed potatoes mixed with flour and shortening. It is rolled thinner than a tortilla and in the shape of a circle about 12-14 inches in diameter and fried on a skillet. Fresh lefse with a little butter and sugar is my favorite (my wife makes the best lefse I've ever eaten). The only bad thing is that if you ate enough of it you'd weigh 400 pounds.

Another favorite is klubb, a Norwegian potato dumpling that usually has a small piece of ham in the center. My family calls them krubb, but I guess the correct Norwegian name is klubb. I eat them with butter and salt and pepper. My wife eats them with pancake syrup (I've heard Norwegians say either way is traditional). My mother makes them every Christmas and so they have become a traditional Christmas dish at our house.

Of course there is kuchen, the German breakfast pastry that's sort of like fruit pie with a sweet egg and usually cream concoction mixed in the fruit. What's not to like?

Another good one is fleischkuechle, a German dish, which is, in reality, sort of a deep fried hamburger. I'll tell you about my first exposure to fleischkuechle. The summer I graduated from high school, the town of Center had what they thought was a good Legion baseball team. They were undefeated at mid summer. Center has a celebration at that time of the summer called Old Settlers Days. They thought it would be great to invite the Steele Legion team out to Center and administer a good beating on us as part of their celebration. They obviously didn't know who they were dealing with. They may have had delusions of grandeur or at the least just plain delusions. We went out to Center and kicked the snot out of them, winning the game by about 17-0. Anyway, what I'm getting at (other than bragging about our baseball prowess and there will be more bragging later), was that after the game the city mothers, much to our delight fed us fleischkuechle. It really is good.

The last food I'll mention is knoephla soup. My hunting buddy Mark's mother made really good knoephla soup. Her swan left a little to be desired, but that's another story. It is potato cream soup with little dough dumplings that the Germans call knoephlas. I could probably live on the stuff.

Oh yeah, don't believe anything you've heard about the Norwegian lutefisk. It's not even that good. Just say "NO".

I don't think any other movie has had as profound an effect on a person as Alfred Hitchcock's thriller, "The Birds", had on my older sister Lennis. We originally watched it at a neighbor's place when it first came on television. I don't think she even finished watching it. When we got home that night my brother Rob and I went upstairs to go to bed and as soon as we got up there we started screaming. Lennis went berserk, and later when she found out we were messing with her, she would have liked to have killed us. For the rest of her life she was never comfortable around live birds, whether it was full-grown chickens or baby ducks. Years later, when she was home for the summer during her college years, she was out windrowing grain to prepare it for combining. At mid morning she drove in the yard. Dad and I were getting combines ready to roll for harvest. Dad went and talked to her, asking her if she had broken down. She was clearly agitated and told dad she wasn't going back out there until he got rid of those seagulls. Hitchcock would have been proud.

We discovered skateboards (believe it or not, we started the sport of skateboarding, not the x-generation) and the words "crash and burn" entered our vocabulary. We never had any areas to skateboard like they do today. We had to improvise. There was nothing like cruising down the sidewalk, taking a turn and heading down a driveway, hitting a rock and getting launched out in the street. We were in a constant state of body disrepair. We didn't have helmets and knee, elbow and hand pads. It just made our growing up process a little more complicated. But it was fun. As Eddie Christiansen (my partner Bob's dad) always said, "Any experience that doesn't kill you just makes you stronger". We were really getting strong. Like everything else we did as youngsters; we rode skateboards just for fun. In this day and age, you can actually make a good living skateboarding. Something about that just doesn't seem right. It's just a toy.

In our youth, television was in its infancy, and we had no idea what a powerful influence it would become. My very first memories of television are when we lived in a little house in Driscoll when I was less than four years old. Saturday nights were bath nights and we would bathe in a galvanized metal bathtub in a corner of the living room while watching "The Lawrence Welk Show".

There are a couple things that were on TV during our youth that you don't see at all today. The first one was the early morning sign-on test pattern. It wasn't too uncommon for one of us kids to roll out early in the morning. We would head out to the living room, turn the television on, sit there and watch the snow until the test pattern came on and then sit and watch that. Eventually programming came on. We didn't mind, it was so new to us that it was all so fascinating. The second thing was the waving flag and the playing of the national anthem when the station signed-off and shut down it's transmitter, usually from midnight to six or seven AM. Today, all stations stay on the air 24 hours a day whether they have programming on our not.

Other than the show that I associated with my bath time, I don't specifically remember when I really started to watch television. Television entered our lives slowly but surely. At the advent of TV in the Steele area there wasn't a cable system and only two over the air stations. So little to choose from and my big sister and I still managed to fight over what we were going to watch!

I do remember some of the shows that I watched on Saturdays a little later. Who could forget "Out of the blue of the western sky comes, (big plane engine noise) Sky King!" At some point during my youth, the Roadrunner and his nemesis

Wiley E. Coyote made their debut. We watched Lassie save Tim so many different ways, that kid should have had a leash on! Back in those days, Saturday mornings were and they continue to be the kid's favorite viewing time, with its cartoons and kid oriented shows, like the ones listed above.

Among my favorites as a kid, other than the previously mentioned Saturday morning shows, was "Highway Patrol" starring Broderick Crawford. Do you remember the private detective show "Honey West"? It featured one of TV's sexier detectives (Anne Francis), at least until Angie Dickinson's "Police Woman". Another favorite was the spy show, "The Man From Uncle". "Gunsmoke" was my Dad's favorite. Do you remember the predecessor to the "Beverly Hillbillies"; a show called "The Real McCoys"? "I Love Lucy", believe it or not, was already in syndication when I first remember watching it. The game shows that were on TV in those days paled in sophistication compared to today, but we watched "I've Got A Secret" and "What's My Line" religiously. Family shows like "Leave It To Beaver, "Ozzie and Harriet" and "Father Knows Best" were among the most popular shows on television. The first animated prime time TV show, "The Flintstones" with Fred and Wilma, Barney and Betty, was a lot of fun. Yeah, someday, maybe Fred will win the fight and that cat will stay out for the night.

The special effects of today did not exist yet, even during the time "Batman" was on the air in 1966-68. We all remember the original "Superman" series. They were trying to be serious but even to my kid eyes the "flying" and the "x-ray vision" were really hokey. TV's longest running sci-fi show was "Voyage to the Bottom of the Sea". It was on television well before the sci-fi show that we all remember best, "Star Trek". "Star Trek" was the first show with real special effects. If you watch an episode of "Star Trek" today, the special effects are really weak. It's amazing, at the time they seemed so real! It inspired probably the most popular series of movies created (other than the James Bond movies), the Star Wars series. Beyond that, it also inspired an entire industry that is producing memorabilia for the "Trekies", as hardcore Star Trek fans are called. Live well and prosper.

The first real popular pre-CNN news show was the Huntley-Brinkley Report. Watching that show was like sitting in front of your Grandpa, while he talked about what was going on around town. Today's cynicism was still years away. You trusted them. I can still hear them sign off with their familiar "Goodnight David, Goodnight Chet". To my Dad those words meant only one thing; it was SUPPERTIME! Which brings up an important question; just when did supper become dinner? Did we vote on that?

One day, in the early 60's, I'm thinking 1963 or 64, I came home from school and Harry had brought over a new TV set. I turned it on, it was nice, but I didn't think anything was wrong with the old set. Then the show I was watching ended at 4:30, and I don't remember what the next show was but when it came on, WOW, it was in color! The color era had begun!

In the fall of 1961, Roger Maris and Mickey Mantle, both of the New York Yankees, were locked in a home run race. You have to keep in mind, we lived in a baseball town (we'll talk more about this a little later), and this was a big deal to a lot of us kids. Both of them were challenging Babe Ruth's record of 60 home runs in a season, as well as trying to lead Major League Baseball in round trippers for the year. When school started, I couldn't check for radio reports of their exploits. Dad worked downtown at Dave Albright's John Deere dealership. I stopped there every day on the way home from school during September. I couldn't wait! I had to ask Dad, Mike (Karen's boyfriend, Michael's dad) or Walt if either Maris or Mantle had hit a home run that day. Of course at the end of the season Maris pulled away from Mantle and on the last day of the season hit his 61st home run, to break the old record.

I think Mantle finished with 54 home runs. It was a very exciting time!

The Fourth of July rivaled Christmas as our favorite holiday. Why? FIREWORKS!! In those days, you were free to shoot fireworks almost anywhere. And we did shoot them. We learned how to blow up beer cans, how to launch tin cans way up in the air or how to booby trap car and house doors. It was lucky for us we didn't know how dangerous they were or some of us would have gotten hurt.

A week or two before the 4th, when I was in my 11th year, I was sitting in the family car just across the street from Tolly's Grocery store, where Mom was picking up a couple things. Just a couple doors to the west of the grocery store was the building that housed Mullen Drug, until that spring, when it had merged with Yanken Drug. The building was being used as the local fireworks stand that summer. The drug store building was one of several buildings that were torn down several years later to make room for the new bank. The building sat in what is now the bank's parking lot. A few older kids were shooting bottle rockets back and forth across the street. Now when they designed the bottle rocket, the onboard guidance system left a little to be desired. One of those rockets went a little off course, and you guessed it, right through the doorway, into the stacked up fireworks and BAM, it was the darndest thing I ever saw. You would think that many dollars worth of fireworks would have made a better show. But they mostly just popped, fizzled and smoked.

If you were to open a fireworks stand and you could name it anything you wanted, what would it be? I was watching a movie recently and in one scene the main characters were coming out of a fireworks store. The name of the store on the sign above the door was "Three Finger Freddies Fireworks". That just cracked me up. What a perfect name for a fireworks store!

North Dakota has done it damnedest to squash the use of fireworks. I really think our legislators and our county and city commissioners need to get off their high horses and let the kids have a little fun. I think they must lie awake nights thinking of bonehead reasons why they shouldn't be allowed. If it isn't because of noise, it's too dry, or someone is going to get hurt. They've got a dozen of them. All of those same factors have always been there, and we seemed to do okay.

When Dave got out of the implement business, Dad and Walt took over the John Deere franchise in Steele for about 5 years in the mid sixties. That created a new chore or two for the oldest kids. One of the chores was that we learned the joy of inventorying the stock down to the last nut and bolt. There were a surprising number of different things to inventory in a John Deere dealership.

But, on the fun side, we annually celebrated what were called John Deere Days. It was almost like a new holiday. The purpose of John Deere Days was to introduce the new model year of "The Long Green Line" (John Deere equipment is green and yellow). As part of the celebration of John Deere days, they always had free food for everyone who wanted to stop at the store. I loved the baked beans out of the big pot; the sandwiches and the home made pickles. The store was always filled with crowds of people (crowds is a relative term, I'm talking 25-30 people at a time). In a small town, if you offered free food, virtually everyone in town would eventually show up. But the thing I liked most about John Deere Days was the George Gobel (and his wife, spooky old Alice) movie that the John Deere Corporation had made for John Deere Days every year. George Gobel was a comedian who was most well known in country circles and made a lot of guest appearances on variety shows, including many appearances on the "Johnny Carson Show". Later in his career he was a semi-regular on the game show "Hollywood Squares". So the John Deere movies were not his only claim to fame. They used to show the film in the old city auditorium (this was after the Roxy theater days). There was always a big crowd in attendance. In Steele the same rule applied with a free movie as with free food. If it's free we will all come. It's not that they were all cheapskates, they were fiscally responsible. While there was very little chance that 'Lonesome George' would be nominated for an Academy Award for his performance in them, those George Gobel (and spooky old Alice) movies were a lot of fun!

One other thing, during the time that Dad and Walt ran the John Deere shop, the store won a sales contest within the company. The prize was an all-expenses paid trip to Illinois to tour the John Deere manufacturing facilities. Included with the trip were airline tickets to fly there. I don't know who was more excited about the trip, Mom and Dad or us kids, although we weren't the ones going. While they were gone, our Aunt Marlene came and stayed with us. We could hardly wait until Mom and Dad got home to tell us about it. I remember them telling us about their flight, the first that anyone in our family had been on. They told us about going through the clouds and ending up way above them, miles above the ground. Miles above the ground! That seemed so farfetched. I couldn't even imagine being so high up in the sky. Air travel was something I would learn more about a little later in my life.

In late 1962, Mom and Dad had bought a new car, a 1963 Chevy Impala. The next summer, Mom decided we should see a little bit more of the world. So we planned an adventure. We decided we were going all the way to Yellowstone National Park! Pretty heady stuff for kids that had never been west of Bismarck.

The first day of our trip, we drove all the way to Miles City, Montana (about 310 or 320 miles west). That night, for the first time in our lives we stayed in a motel. Specifically the "Sunset Motel". After we had a picnic in the local park, (there were no McDonalds to be found in those days) we checked into the motel. In the bathroom of the motel room, I found a thick disposable paper bath or shower mat with the words Sunset Motel and the profile of a cowboy printed on it. I took possession of that mat and kept it for years. All kids have different interests and mine just happened to be mom and pop motels. What's so unusual about that? Many years later my older sister and her family lived in Miles City. When we visited them, the route to their home took us by the Sunset Motel. It was still operating, although since the interstate highway was built, it was no longer anywhere near the mainstream of travel.

Once we got in the park we made all the tourist stops. Yellowstone Park has so many stinky mud pits and steaming geysers. After a while everything turns into a blur because of the sheer amount of things to view. If you stop at a hundred of them, there is always one more. I remember that there were a lot of traffic jams because of all the elk, black and cinnamon bears and buffalo. I've been to Yellowstone Park three times over the years, but it will never be a favorite of mine. There are just too many people. I'll never forget, on one of our trips we were following a car that suddenly hit the brakes and stopped in the middle of the active driving lane of the highway. I had to take quick evasive action to not hit them. Why did they stop? On the river flowing along side the highway there were three pelicans swimming! They had to have some pictures of the pelicans.

Yellowstone Park is one of the real natural wonders in the United States, and everyone should visit the park at least once in their lifetime. It's too bad that they don't have some kind of national visit schedule that assigns different years for different groups of states. In North Dakota's year, of course, all the visitors from North Dakota would either be related to or at the least know everyone else from North Dakota visiting the park. We could all go in June and it would be just like a big family reunion.

One of the really amazing things we've all seen in Yellowstone Park are the crazy wildlife photographers. They go about it like this is their job and if they get a really good picture they'll almost certainly win a Pulitzer Prize. There are signs posted everywhere warning people to stay away from wildlife. Inevitably when an animal appeared along or on the road, people were piling out of their cars trying to get the ultimate close up. We've never seen anyone attacked when we've been there but we've read about it many times. It just proves the old adage, "there's an idiot born every minute"! They may have said 'sucker' when that phrase was coined, but 'idiot' fits just as well.

Yellowstone Park had its worst forest fires in recorded history in the late 80's. The park policy at that time was to let forest fires burn for a more natural sequence of events. That followed a long period of fire suppression. A natural sequence of events is the fire burns through any given area and accomplishes two things. First it removes the forest canopy that shades everything else and that allows ground dwelling grasses and shrubs to grow prolifically. The second thing is that the fire causes pine cones to burst and naturally the forest floor is covered with tree seed. When the seeds sprout, the forest's regeneration is under way. What they didn't count on was that all the previous years of suppressing fires had allowed a huge amount of flammable material to accumulate on the ground. Because of all that material, the fires burned so hot that they sterilized the soil and killed all the pine seeds. So in many areas, ten years later there was absolutely no regrowth of any kind. Here is where my old buddy Tim stepped in. Tim is a big game outfitter in the fall and because of that he has the resources the Park Service needed. They hired him to pack in on packhorses huge numbers of tree seedlings to be planted along the trails to give hikers the appearance that the forest was regrowing. Kind of a Yellowstonegate. The Park Service was covering up the mistake they made of allowing the fires to continue burning. The real mistake that was made was to suppress fires for a long time, allowing flammable material to build up on the forest's floor. So, maybe the fires were a necessary evil.

A couple years later we were traveling again, this time we were headed south with my Grandma Nelson as a passenger. We drove to Oklahoma to visit my Uncle Dale and his family at his station at Vance Air Force base near Enid, Oklahoma. He and his family lived in base housing at that time. I met my very first black kids during this trip. I was right; they weren't any different than us. While we were there, the kids in the base housing area had a baseball game going on constantly during the daylight hours. If you wanted to play you just joined a side and played. When you had to leave you just left. There didn't seem to be a conclusion to the game, it went on and on only stopping at dark and then would start back right back up the next morning, weather permitting.

Also, we got to watch "Super Girl", who was really my cousin Diana in disguise, dive off the arm of their easy chair and sofa in an attempt to fly. She failed miserably. She was incredible. She really believed she could fly and was constantly diving off furniture and would flop right on her face. It had to hurt!

On the way home, it came as a surprise to us, but we got to meet someone famous. It was the first time I had ever met a TV star. We stopped in Dodge City, Kansas and there we met Ken Curtis, 'Festus' of the TV show Gunsmoke. He happened to be making a personal appearance in the modern Dodge Cities reproduction of the original Dodge City while we were going through town.

When we got older we drank a little beer, and we did enjoy it. It was a rite of passage and was more or less socially acceptable in those days, if we kept it out of sight. I realize that this a very controversial subject in this day and age, but recreational drinking was a very real part of our social lives. I'm not going to sit here and lie to you, telling you that nothing irresponsible ever happened, because things did happen that shouldn't have. Alcohol is a dangerous drug and its use in excess is not acceptable.

Sadly, the only deaths of young people in our town (except for Tony Meier who died of a congenital heart problem) that I can recall were the result of their being hit by a drunk driver. When something like that happens, if you're human, you've got to give some serious thought to giving up drinking alcohol. A young person's life is more important than drinking a few beers. The reality of the situation is that if you don't abuse alcohol you aren't part of the problem, so it really doesn't matter what you do. You can't control the drinking and driving of everyone else. It's just a curse on our society; our freedom allows anyone to drink alcoholic beverages. But we have to rely on someone else's common sense to not drink and drive. So, other than stricter law enforcement, there really isn't a solution to this problem. In the end you just have to look out for yourself.

During our years in high school, we didn't have any trouble finding things to do, other than sports. One of our favorite activities was the 'hayrides' that we went on. We would find a bale pile, it could be anywhere or anybody's, and we didn't discriminate. We would throw a few bales in a pickup box, jump in. get comfortable and cruise around, just talking, for hours.

We lit a bonfire once in a while. We'd pull a car with an 8-track tape player in close and we would play a little CCR, Beach Boys, Mamas and the Papas or whatever else we had in our tape cases. We weren't real big on bonfires because we didn't like to send an invitation (the light of the fire) to the sheriff. There was one place northwest of town that worked pretty well for a fire. It was a dense; circular shaped grove of trees and because of that was hard to spot. One of our favorite places to gather was an old farmhouse that we discovered still had power to its fuse panel. We blacked out the windows and heated it a little with the stove oven in the kitchen.

In the summers we would pile in Tommy Janke's full size (There weren't any mini-vans in existence then.) van and go to buck ($1) night (Wednesday) at the Starlite drive in theater. We also found some more unique ways to recreate. One evening we were up northwest of town and we noticed it was a full moon night. It was so light out that a few of us decided we were going to stack hay, which we did for 2 or 3 hours. We moved the stack frame twice and made a total of three stacks. I'm sure the farmer was surprised the next day. We tried to do a good job and not leave a mess, but who knew for sure, after all, we were working by moonlight.

The parents of one of my best friends, Tom, had a cabin on Lake Isabel (10 miles southeast of Steele). Tom and I and a few other buddies were on Steele's amateur baseball team. The team played most of its games on Sunday. We would play our one or two games on Sunday afternoon. And then, a few times a summer we would have an 8-gallon keg of beer in a wash tub of ice, so it was chilled and waiting for us at the cabin after the game or games. We played some really great football games and also put on some really good floorshows, featuring "The Singing Fools". The night usually ended up with three or four (we usually slept at the cabin) of us taking turns laying under the spigot and drinking as much as we could in an attempt to finish the keg.

Tom had a 63 Chevy convertible back in the 1970ish time period. One night there were six of us riding in his car. I don't remember what we were up to other than we were driving on the old highway (US 10) on our way from Sterling to Steele. Anyway, it was dark out. Tom was driving and I think Ron was sitting in the middle of the front seat next to Tom. I was sitting directly behind Tom and was in an animated conversation with him about something, so he was turned around talking to me more than he was looking forward. If Ron hadn't been watching the road the headlines in the Bismarck Tribune the next day would have been something like "Several Kidder County Men Injured In High Speed Collision With Cow". Like I said, Tom was turned around, I was looking forward, and suddenly completely across the eastbound lane there was a full-grown cow, Ron grabbed the wheel and jerked it so we missed the cow. Tom, in a huff, turned around and hollered at Ron something about him trying to kill us all. It took at least three of us to convince him there was a cow on the road, he never saw it.

Tom is a great guy and a great friend. To this day, we still spend time together, usually fishing or at college football games. One winter day, four of us, including Tom, were over on Crystal Springs trying to ice fish. We weren't doing very well. But, all was not lost; we had some beer along. So someone got the bright idea we should draw cards and the low card had to chug a beer. We had just barely started and Tom had to go to the bathroom. So what did the other three fine upstanding young men do when Tom got out of the car? We stacked the deck of course. Tom got back in and immediately he was on a losing streak. He never caught on. We had to pull over twice on the way home because Tom had to throw up. With friends like that, who needs enemies? A funny thing about Tom, if he had to throw up, someone always had to hold his hand.

My first date with my wife occurred at least partly because of my taste for beer. I was 20 years old and in my cousin's bar in Driscoll, when a deputy sheriff pulled into town. Cousin Bruce had warned me that if the law showed up in town I would have to get out, so he asked me to leave. Gail Gunderson, a pretty dark-haired, brown-eyed eastern North Dakota girl, who was teaching in the Driscoll elementary school, also happened to be in the bar. I think she was having a beer with her housemate, Rita. She was a little more than a year older than I was, so she was there legally. She was watching when Bruce asked me to leave. We weren't exactly strangers. We had met once before at a get together at the house that she and Rita lived in just west of Driscoll. With me being the handsome devil that I am, she must have been intrigued and volunteered to escort me out of the bar. What a romantic setting for a first date! There is one thing about that night I'll never forget (other than the pretty girl I was with). There was a big beautiful full moon. With that fine start to our relationship, we, of course, were married about a year later. Thirty-two years later we're still married. She's the love of my life.

My senior year in high school, I entered into a relationship with a young lady, one of my high school classmates, that was unlike any relationship I'd ever had with a girl. She was a girl who I had known for about seven or eight years and she became a good friend. Her name was Carla. She was definitely not what I would consider to be a girlfriend. It had never occurred to me, a sexist idiot, that having a female 'friend' was a possibility. Sadly, girls, up until that time were only to be dated. There was also a little bit of a status thing involved. It seemed like the prettier the girl you dated, the more status you had. And there was a constant battle of the sexes going on. On the boy's side, we were always pushing to have sex. On the girl's side they resisted, hoping for a boy who would listen to them, be romantic, and be sensitive to their feelings. In the middle of that battlefield there was Carla and myself and our relationship. Carla and I communicated better than I did with anyone else that was in my life at the time. Until I met my wife, I had never known a girl so well. It never really entered my mind that we should date, its not like she wasn't a very attractive young lady, but for some reason we never did. Sadly, shortly after college she left the area (she now lives out in the Olympia, Washington area) and I haven't seen her for many years. What a revolutionary idea, a girl that's a friend.

I know we've already touched on this subject in another light, but one of the few things I don't like about North Dakota, is that everyone knows everyone else. Every where you turned, someone knew you. Sometimes too much familiarity comes back to bite you. Most of the people in town even knew what vehicle you drove. You could never get away with anything. If we were drinking beer or raising any kind of a ruckus in the area, our parents knew about it before we even got home. Heck it probably showed up in the Steele Ozone's (the local paper) social columns the next issue.

Speaking of raising a ruckus, in the spring of 1970, about 30 or so Steele-Dawson seniors boarded a school bus and headed south to South Dakota and the Black Hills on a 3-day adventure. It was called 'the senior trip' but really should have been called Marv's Teenage Behavior Education weekend. Marv was a teacher and coach who was the main chaperone for our senior trip. He and his wife Irene were raising five kids. We took it upon ourselves to teach him about all kinds of things that his future teenagers would try to pull on him. I know that sounds like a giant responsibility, but we more than happy to help. I remember him coming on the bus one morning and just chewing us out over our previous night's behavior. It was good, he was experiencing new things. We were doing our job.

I don't know if a senior trip is still part of the program at Steele, but we sure had a blast. We didn't do anything terrible, we just worked hard to get Marv his masters degree in teenage behavior. It didn't take us long to find a beer buyer because we had brought our own along. In those days South Dakota would sell 3.2% alcohol beer to 19 year olds and classmate Donny was a two year red shirt (was held back two times in grade school) who was actually just about 20! So the trip during the day was visiting Mt Rushmore, Reptile Gardens and the anti-gravity tourist traps, and at night we drank a little beer, played a little poker and courted young ladies. We created a lot of great memories, putting the finishing touches on our high school experience.

On one of the evenings of the trip, classmate Doug and I snuck out of our room. I think it was the last night of our trip. Amazingly we found another bunch of North Dakota kids in a different motel. The kids we found were from Fullerton, North Dakota (a small town, between Oakes and Ellendale nearly on the South Dakota border in the south central part of the state). What was even more amazing was that one of them was a young lady, Charlene, who just by chance, would be my sister's dormitory roommate at North Dakota State University that coming fall quarter. Once again, North Dakota is such a small state! Doug picked up the Bible in their motel room and started a comedy monologue with a line out of the bible. I don't know the chapter and verse that he quoted, but what I remember him "reading" was "Jesus tied his ass to a tree and walked six miles". He cracked them up! It turned into a real fun evening. I even went on a moonlight walk with one of the young ladies, Jane, and somehow managed to steal a kiss or two.

Among the important things we learned in high school, we learned how to have a good time. Most of us also learned not to abuse ourselves by over doing a good time. I'm not sure that many people realize how important it is to learn both of those lessons. I saw far too many kids that just fell apart when they got away from home because they were so inexperienced socially.

I used to collect baseball cards when I was a young boy. Back then it was a hobby. Today for most people who collect cards, it's an avocation. I was a New York Yankee fan so they were the ones I concentrated on. I had almost all of the 1961 Yankees. I must have missed the article in the Card Collectors Newsletter explaining to everyone how valuable baseball cards would be in the future.

Do you remember the way kids used to clip baseball cards to the fenders of their bikes to make noise when the spokes hit them? I pretty much destroyed every card I owned doing that. They weren't worth anything anyway, were they? I wonder how many thousands of dollars I ground up with my bike. Can you imagine putting Mickey Mantle's rookie card on your bike fender? I'm sure I did it because I did have a 1951 or 1952 Topps Mickey Mantle. I don't remember exactly what year he was a rookie. I do remember trading with Bobby Torbla for it. That was a $20,000 noisemaker. Several years ago, my son was looking for baseball cards down at the farm. He had a hard time finding any, but he did find one of what must have been my little brother's old ones, George Brett's rookie card, so all was not lost. I just checked the value of that card. It is somewhere in the neighborhood of $80. It was the same thing with comic books! Just who decides what people are going to collect? Whoever it was, I wish they would have included me in their little secret. They're probably sitting there giggling about it.

My brother Rob and I were about 4 years different in age, so I discovered girls well before he did. In my high school years, I would come dragging in during the wee hours of the morning. Rob and I slept in the same bedroom. If it was during hunting season, Rob would have the alarm set for us to get up and go hunting. When I got home, I would shut off the alarm when I went to bed. I don't know why, because it would only net me about 10-15 minutes more sleep. He would wake up anyway. Then, I would also have to endure Rob jumping on me and cussing me out because he just had to go hunting. It's not like anyone was keeping score! The wildlife would still be there. But he wouldn't accept defeat. If I tried to ignore him, he would just continue tormenting me until I got up. He was relentless and always won out, so we went hunting. It's not that I didn't enjoy hunting but with hormones raging I couldn't turn my back on the young ladies. We would go through the same thing again the next night. As much as I loved to hunt, Rob was well beyond me. He was a hunting fool. At least until a certain young lady entered his life.

My little brother Darin was a very good basketball and baseball player, neither of which occurred by accident. I don't think there was another kid in Steele who was as nuts about sports as he was or worked harder at them than he did. He was shooting baskets as soon as he could get what we called a dodgeball up to the basket. He used to use pillows and other household objects to outfit himself as a baseball catcher; we've got pictures. He was very innovative. As a result of his hard work, as a sophomore and a junior, he was the only one of us boys to play in not just one but two state basketball tournaments. There was another tall thin boy, Colin, a year older than Darin who was also a great athlete. We always said from the time they were in grade school that when Colin was a senior and Darin a junior, they were going to take the Steele-Dawson basketball team to state. They did it one better by also going as a junior and a sophomore.

Darin was also involved in the infamous "crappy boot" incident when he was a little younger and had just started to hunt. This incident happened one day over at the fenceline, pass shooting geese. Darin told Rob he had to go to the bathroom, maybe thinking that Rob would give him a ride some where. Rob said something like there's paper in the pickup, why are you telling me this. Darin had never pooped anywhere other than on a toilet, but never the less he grabbed the paper and headed for the weeds. After an extremely long time he came limping out of the weeds on one boot, holding the other out in front of him. At the time, we told him we sincerely hoped he would get better with experience, mostly missing himself the next time the urge came along. It was a lead pipe cinch that no other one of us was going to do a demo for him. That's something you've got to learn yourself!

While we're talking about my little brother, we'd better mention another famous (at least it was in our family) incident. It involved Darin's first wife, Patti. We were playing a word game, I think it was called Pictionary. Anyway you had to draw pictures to help your partner guess a particular word. I was Patti's partner and she had drawn the word "elephant" I believe. Patti isn't much of an artist, and when she showed me what she had drawn, it looked just like a man's sex organ. I took one look at it and laughed and told her she was being a little too suggestive. She pulled it back, took another look at it and then discovered that that's exactly what it looked like. It took quite a while to get back to the game. Patti was a pretty straight-laced girl, one of the "P" kids that we'll talk about in the next chapter. I didn't realize someone could turn that shade of red while blushing.

I've got to mention one other thing that happened to me when I was young. This incident may have happened to someone else also, or maybe I was the only idiot out there. When I was about six or so, I was with Dad down in the basement of our house in Steele. Dad was digging around and he found an old radio. He plugged it in to see if it would work. After a few seconds warm up time it came on. It was playing a song I had heard on the car radio just the other day. That mystified me. How could this old radio play a current song? There was a little information gap there. Dad explained to me about radio stations and transmitting signals. Car radios and other sets at home don't contain the music, they receive it. I never would have guessed.

CHAPTER 5

THE NEIGHBORHOOD

When we were young, we would get up on a summer morning and look out the window and if the sun was shining, just smile. Who knew what the day was going to bring? The chances were better than nine out of ten that we were going to enjoy it. We would pull on our clothes, head down to the kitchen and get energized for the day. Then we were off, headed for another day of adventure. Maybe today we would conquer that tree, get that dog on the next block to quit barking and play fetch with us, finish that fort in the chokecherry patch, go eat pizza at Karen's or maybe none or all of the above. Maybe we would find an interesting rock, make spears to fight dragons or build a racecar with those wheels we found. We went as far as our imaginations and the skills of a kid would take us. And we would love every minute of it. The same scene was repeated a thousand times all over the upper midwest in small town America. Our parents never worried if we didn't show up for lunch. They understood we were probably too busy fighting Indians to come home and eat. They knew our stomachs would eventually bring us home, they always did. That was summer on the northern plains!

When we lived in town, our neighborhood was about a block and a half in size, a very small world to an adult, but to us it was as large and varied as an amusement park. The local blacksmith shop and the owner Ed's house formed the northern border of our world. On the southern border was the local doctor's house and the Lutheran parsonage. On the west edge was the Methodist parsonage (we were a very religious bunch of rugrats) and on the east was, Laura and Eva Fogderud's, the spinster sister's house. Their yard was the neighborhood big woods, and it occasionally served as our hideout from Pastor Kinzer, the earthy minister and one of the chief targets of our abuse. Also to the east was the family home of our neighborhood big sister, Karen. Karen's mothers yard contained an old garage where, as we noted earlier, Karen helped us stage the productions of the neighborhood acting troupe. Next to it was an old garage that was packed with the possessions of a former neighbor, Mrs. Vinje. Her husband had been the Kidder County States Attorney for 22 years. We never knew Mrs. Vinje; she was gone before we took control of the neighborhood. In the middle of the block was Dr. Z's garden, usually a bunch of weeds. Next to it was the local athletic field, actually the backyard of the Lutheran parsonage. Our yard was in the middle just north of Dr. Z's garden. It was the neighborhood zoo. My younger brother Rob was the zookeeper. It contained dogs and cats of course, but also had jackrabbits, gophers, owls, ducks and various other reptilian and avian creatures.

I learned something about our neighborhood while researching some of the history of Steele. Steele's first telephone exchange was in our neighborhood. It was in the house where the Fogderud sisters lived. When the sisters bought the building and made it their home, they took out the switchboard. By the time we lived there the phones no longer were manually switched, at least in town. Since we've mentioned them, one thing about the sisters that I thought was a little odd; they never came out of their house. I don't ever remember seeing them out in their yard. I knew that they lived there only because everyone said they did.

When I was quite small, one of my Mom's younger brothers joined the Air Force and ended up stationed at an Air Force base near Fort Worth, Texas. There he met and married a wonderful, pretty Latino lady who has been a treasured member of our family for all these years. It wasn't too long after they were married that they had a daughter, Carrie, who of course wasn't too different in age from me. For many years while my uncle was in the Air Force, he, my aunt and their young family used to spend the bulk of his leave back here in North Dakota during the summers. When my young cousin was old enough she used to follow me around telling me she loved me. She was relentless, and used to embarrass me in front of the neighborhood gang. Of course, a few years later I would have loved to have a pretty, dark-haired, brown-eyed girl follow me around and tell me she loved me. But at the time I was more concerned about having a more conventional relationship with my cousin. But, of course, we did grow up, me included, and things changed. The little pest, Carrie, grew up to be a wonderful, pretty woman who became a great friend as well as a cousin.

The dog we had at that time was a little "yapper" that went by the name of Tippy (he had a black tip on his tail). Tippy was truly part of the family, and a recognized member of our neighborhood. He wandered our block at will, but never left it, and of course everyone knew him. Tippy had a morning ritual that he carried out faithfully every day. At midmorning he would go to the backdoor of Dr. Z's house and bark once or twice. The doctor's wife, Slava, would be expecting him and would come out with a piece of Polish sausage for his breakfast. He would stay and visit for a minute or two and come home. One day Tippy went back for a second helping, but after Slava chastised him for being greedy, he never tried it again. When Dr. Z would sit out in their yard in a lawn chair in the evening, Tippy often went over to visit briefly, and after he said hi would come home. Who says dogs can't reason? I know, I've read about Pavlov and his dogs. He would say they don't think, that what Tippy did was a conditioned response taught by giving a reward, but I like to think Tippy knew what he was doing.

Interestingly enough, Tippy was chasing a car through the alley one day and he collapsed and died. Too much polish sausage?

Our yard had a tire swing that was tied to a branch high up in an old cottonwood tree. My friends and I called it the "Eric Launcher". Why? Well, we were always told to be careful when pushing younger kids so we wouldn't get them too high. One day, a neighbor, Ricky and I were pushing each other on the swing. His little brother, Eric, was watching us and complaining that he wanted to ride too. So we obliged and let him climb in. We started pushing him and he was hollering at us to really get him high. We were happy to do that, until, at the highest spot in its travel, Eric was suddenly launched far out into Mom's garden. He landed with an "oomph" and a cloud of dust and, of course, started crying which instantly attracted mothers from all directions. Ricky and I got the heck out of Dodge. We did get the lecture about little kids and the tire swing one more time.

When I was about 6 or so, someone moved into the little house just north of Karen's Mom's house. A couple days later, it must have been a Sunday, because I think I was walking home from Church school, I walked by that house, and there, big as you please sat my tricycle right by the front steps. Getting into an immediate huff, I grabbed the trike and headed home, noticing on the way that my handlebars, which had been loose, had been tightened up. Well, in the next day or two the thief and I had a confrontation. It turned out to be a blonde boy that was the same age as me. He claimed he was just fixing my trike for me. I had to admit that was true. To make a long story short, Billy (the blonde boy) and I became good friends and experienced sports, school, and girls (among other things) together over the next 11 or 12 years. He has also stayed in North Dakota and we very occasionally run into each other and talk about the old days back in Steele. Incidentally, not only did Bill become the best baseball player in a baseball town; the summer we graduated from high school, he was the best player in the state, period.

One of our next door neighbors was a young boy 3 or 4 years younger than me that suffered from allergies and so he was always sniffing and wiping his nose on his sleeve. One day I was outside and I noticed Bobby (the sniffer) throwing something up in one of their trees. He would throw it, it would fall back down, and he would pick it up and throw it again. I walked over to investigate and saw that there was a hornet's nest in the tree that Bobby was trying to knock down. I quickly advised him not to do that as I was retreating. A few minutes later I was in the house and heard Bobby hollering, looked out the window and saw him running away flailing his arms around his head. The next time I saw him, I had to keep myself from laughing because Bobby's head looked like a basketball sitting on his shoulders, it was so swollen up from the hornet stings. Another life lesson learned the hard way! He's lucky the hornet stings didn't kill him. Bobby left the state when he grew up, and moved to the Deep South of all places. He thankfully grew out of his allergies.

Bobby had a lot of issues. He came from a nice family, (Bobby's older brother Kenny was a great guy) but he was a constant tormentor of some of the younger neighborhood kids. As an example, one day I had to get on his case about picking on my little sister. How could a 5-year-old girl be threatening to a kid his age? Somehow he imagined she could be! My little sister was kind of a spitfire. She probably retaliated for something he had started, and that really set him off. I don't mean to make excuses, but with his allergies and the constant stream of snot coming out of his nose he was often shunned or made fun of. Maybe he was just taking out his frustrations.

Anyway we were never quite able to tame the kid while he lived in our neighborhood.

One day after school, a long simmering feud erupted into a battle between the Hoff brothers and my brother Rob and our friend and future hunting comrade Mark. Now Rob and Mark were two of Bobby's neighborhood whipping boys, but when Bobby seen the battle going on with the Hoff boys, he waded in on the side of the neighborhood boys and they routed the Hoffs. By golly, no one was going to come into his neighborhood and mess with his whipping boys!

Our western neighbors were the Kinzers who were not a typical family in any sense of the word. I don't remember where they came from. We kids knew that privately Reverend Kinzer wasn't exactly the model minister. We had heard the Reverend use some pretty colorful language, at least within the parsonage walls. How did we know that? No, we didn't have hidden microphones in their house. They just had the windows open a lot of the time in the summer, something that Rev, Kinzer apparently didn't take into consideration before he let fly with the colorful language. You could set out in our yard and listen to him chastise Frankie and the rest of the kids, using words that we weren't allowed to use. If he didn't want us to hear, he should have shut his windows, or shut up. To the church going public, his image was very much a minister.

The girls in the Kinzer family were quiet almost to a fault. One of their daughters was a really nice, but terribly quiet and shy girl, named Bernice, the spitting image of her mother. She was the oldest. Next in age was another daughter, Judy. Judy was a very pretty girl, who was also quiet, and a little devious. You never knew what was really going on in her mind. They also had a third daughter, Mary Kate who was just a baby when they were our neighbors. She was the most bowlegged kid I've ever seen. Their only son, Frankie, poor Frankie, was always in his dad's doghouse. Frankie always thought of himself as a little bit of a clown, and he was always looking for attention.

Frankie also didn't have enough common sense to come in from the rain.

One day Mom got a call from Mrs. Kinzer. She said Frankie and Judy were coming over with some bananas. It seems that when no one was at home at our place, the two of them had walked into our house and helped themselves to some bananas. So after Mom had talked with Mrs. Kinzer, she met Judy and Frankie at the door and acted like she knew nothing about why they were there. Judy handed Mom the bananas they had brought, telling her that Frankie had entered our house while we weren't there and had taken some. She didn't want to admit being part of it. She didn't mind hanging her brother out to dry though. Sisters, can't live with them, can't live without them.

My brother Rob and Frankie were actually pretty close to the same age. I don't know exactly why, but putting Frankie in front of Rob was like waving a red flag in a bull's face. Rob took it upon himself as a personal challenge to get Frankie to do the most outrageous thing he could think of. To be honest, Frankie wasn't the brightest bulb in the string; he never seemed to figure out Rob was jerking him around. As I said, Frankie was always trying to be a clown and Rob took advantage of that. He would always convince Frankie that he was being so funny when he was really doing some stupid things (like peeing off their front steps or jumping up and down in mud puddles in the alley). Of course Rev. Kinzer was constantly after Rob to punish him for mistreating Frankie. Rob never did anything to Frankie to physically hurt him, but by the Reverend's reaction, you would have sworn Rob cut off an arm or something.

One day, when Rob was accused of doing something particularly harsh to Frankie, Rev. Kinzer started after Rob on a dead run. Rumor was he tied Frankie to their clothesline pole, but I'm pretty sure he didn't do it. It just may have been one of us older kids. Rob evaded him and as he was running by big sister Karen's house, she grabbed him, took him in their house and hid him under a bed. Rev. Kinzer arrived shortly and went to Karen's door and demanded that she turn over Rob. Karen stood face to face with him and told him to take a hike, earning the undying admiration of all of us. Reverend Kinzler was just not a nice man, something we all recognized. We each did our darndest to aggravate him as much as possible. I'm sure he got tired of dealing with us.

After the Kinzer family left town, the church sold the house, ending a string of minister neighbors. During the 10 or so years, there were the Wehrli's, the Kinzers, and a young single minister I only remember as "Joe" who it seemed always had a girl friend visiting him. A young family bought the house from the church. They had a bunch of young kids and all of their names started with a "P". Let's see there was Patrick, Preston, Patricia, Petina, Priscilla and Penelope. I think that's all of them. Rob always had trouble keeping the kids and their names straight. One day he was telling Mom what one of the "P" kids had done and Mom asked him which one of the kids was he talking about. He got a little flustered while he was telling who it was and said something like "I don't know, it was Penelope or Priscillapy or one of those P names". It was funny, but I guess you had to be there.

Jerome, the father of the "P" kids became the manager of the BEK telephone co-op. He just recently retired. He had a very successful run as manager. During the time he was in charge, he turned it into a fairly large telecommunications company, the largest employer in Steele.

One day when Rob was around 10 years old, he noticed the garage doors to Mrs. Vinje's garage were open. Upon investigation he discovered that Mrs. Vinje's son, Arne, was cleaning out the garage and either hauling away or disposing of her possessions. Rob quickly spotted four old guns and began negotiating their purchase. Shortly thereafter he came trotting back to the house, telling us he needed to borrow $10.

Arne had put a condition on the sale. Dad had to go over to the garage and tell him it was okay for Rob to buy the guns. I don't remember who gave him the money, but he got it, and after Dad gave his blessing he came back with an armful of guns, beginning a life long love affair with shooting, hunting and the outdoors.

As a sidebar to this story, several years later after we had moved out to the farm, I was upstairs in the house and Rob was down in his room. I heard a pop but kind of blew it off. A few minutes later, Rob came upstairs with a sheepish look on his face. It turns out that he was messing with one of the guns he had bought that day in the garage, a 20-gauge shotgun, swinging it up and aiming at a duck pictured on a calendar. He squeezed the trigger, and you got it, it went off obliterating the duck. He thought he could fix it by moving another picture over the hole. Then he went into the bathroom next door to use the facilities, and discovered a huge hole blown in the other side of the wall. He knew then he was in trouble and gave himself up. The only good thing about it was that he did get the duck. But he broke the rule that requires us to always treat a gun as if it is loaded. Of course, nothing like that ever happened again. Once was enough!

I recently learned there is now another interesting telecommunications company in Steele. No, it isn't a phone sex company, don't get started now. The company is known by the initials 'SEI'. One of the services that they provide is taking drive up food orders for a major fast food vendor. They are able to take orders for restaurants all over the country. Amazing, but if you think about it, it is very doable with today's technology. All you need is a phone line and a personal computer.

When the sun went down in the summer, it was time to play our favorite game. We played what is commonly called 'tag', but it was much more fun to play it in the dark. One guy was 'it' and his job was to capture the others. A capture was

accomplished by a touch, whether it was by sneaking up on them or running them down, if you touched them they were captured. The game was over when you captured all the other kids. In the process we ran into fences, clotheslines and lawn ornaments. The neighborhood that was so familiar by day seemed to rise up to get you at night. One night while being heavily pursued I was cornered up against a thick hedge. The only way out was through the hedge. I remember that when I went through it there was a lot of scratching and clawing at my face and it stung. When I got home and looked in the bathroom mirror I was surprised to see I looked like I'd been in an hour-long fight with an angry cat. When my mother saw it she hauled me off to the medicine cabinet. By the time she was through with me, my face looked like an advertisement for Mercurochrome.

When we roamed our small world we didn't have time to go in a house to get a drink or go to the bathroom. That's not really true, we were always afraid we'd miss something if we went. Then there was always the chance that a mother would get a hold of us and send us on an errand or put us to work doing a chore. So, most of the water we drank was from a garden hose somewhere in the neighborhood. We never had a second thought about it. The only thing about the hose was that the water always tasted like, well, "garden hose". It actually would have been neat to have bottled water like they do today. But it was a small price to pay. Dirt or dog saliva was never an issue. If one of us managed to come up with a bottle of pop (not soda, it was pop and it was in a 12 ounce glass bottle), it was passed around to the whole gang. Each guy, in turn took the precaution of "sterilizing" the bottle opening with his shirtsleeve. If one of us was diseased, we all got it. I guess it just made us tougher. When it was empty we took the bottle to the grocery store and traded it for Bazooka bubble gum. As far as going to the bathroom, we boys just got behind any tree. It was a little more complicated for the girls.

One day over at Billy the trike thief's house, we snuck through an outside entry door into their basement (we weren't supposed to be down there). Bill and I were about 9 or 10 years old and my brother Rob who was along with us was about 5 or 6. We found and were investigating some canned vegetables that had been left in the basement when the previous dwellers moved out. We honestly had no idea what was in the jars. Well, we got one open, and we found we had the perfect guinea pig along. We talked Rob into taking a bite. He did take a bite and with in 10-15 seconds Rob was hollering as he ran out the door. Billy and I looked at each other, closed the jar and left the premises. Well my Mom hunted us down in minutes and demanded that Bill and I show her what Rob had eaten. When the investigation was completed, we got a lecture on hot peppers, and we were also told in no uncertain terms that we should **never** use the 'guinea pig' to test anything. Rob's mouth was actually blistered. Aah, life's little lessons.

There were a couple kids in our neighborhood that never or rarely were included in our adventures, they were a brother and a sister from a family on the south side of our neighborhood. No, just because they were from the south, don't assume they were slave owners. Just joking, south, slave owners, get it. Bad joke. The sister was 8 going on 18 years and was always too mature to mess with us (come to think of it she did act like a southern belle). The brother seemed "strange " to the rest of us. He never wanted to join us in boy stuff. It wasn't until he was out of high school that we found out he was gay, one of only a couple gay kids that I knew of from our community. We could get into the whole environmental, parenting or genetic thing, but let's just say that its something that just happens. I don't think there was anything extenuating in his life, he was just gay. On the sad side, he died from AIDS in his early 50's.

When we were kids, about two or three times a year one of our parents would announce at supper that they had been told by someone down town that the "gypsies" were in town. We were to pick all of our stuff up and put it away, because the gypsies would steal anything left out in the open. Of all the times we were told the gypsies were in town, not even once did I ever hear about one of them stealing anything. But it was traditional whenever someone decided there were gypsies around you had to keep your kids in after dark, tie up your dogs, and lock your freezers, cars and houses! We always wanted to see a gypsy, I don't know what we expected them to look like, but I don't think I ever saw one. Then, of course, when we were into our teen-age years, we always wanted to meet a gypsy girl. There were all kinds of rumors floating around about them. In truth they most likely lived only in our collective imaginations.

CHAPTER 6

NORTH DAKOTA WEATHER

In 1966, we witnessed probably the most awesome display of Mother Nature's fury that most North Dakotans have ever seen. Shortly after noon on the first Wednesday of March, 1966, I was an eighth grader sitting on a bus in front of the Steele-Dawson school. The bus I was on was supposed to transport basketball fans 20 miles north to the district high school basketball tournament in Tuttle. It was snowing and the wait was beginning to get a little long. Finally, the high school principal stuck his head in the door of the bus and told us that because of the weather forecast the tournament was being postponed. The first two games of the tournament were played that afternoon. At 1 PM, the Steele-Dawson Pirates won the first game, defeating the Pettibone Warriors. At 2:45 PM, in the second game, Hurdsfield Stags beat the Woodworth Mallards. The basketball team and cheerleaders then made a late afternoon trip back to Steele in heavy snowfall. The tournament was completed the next week. By Thursday morning there were high winds and heavy snow in Steele and the Blizzard of '66 was off and running. School was canceled Thursday and Friday. The Blizzard of '66 was the most punishing weather event that 99% of us have ever seen. None of us have been in a hurricane, but even a hurricane doesn't last for three days. I'm not making light of hurricanes, they are a deadly weather phenomena, but many people, along with huge numbers of livestock perished in this storm. One quick non-weather note, of the four high schools that played those two games on that stormy day 40 years ago, Steele-Dawson is the only high school still open.

We need to make a comment about the comparison of the 1966 blizzard to a hurricane, in particular, the participation of the Federal government in post storm recovery. It's true the property damage that occurred in the blizzard, although significant, paled in comparison to the physical property damage caused by an average hurricane. While the Feds mobilize half of the government and pour in money by the truckload to help in hurricane recovery, federal aid in the aftermath of the '66 snowstorm was pretty much non-existent. There just aren't enough voters up here and although we did get some press, it wasn't much. To be honest, we didn't expect any Federal aid. We would have been embarrassed to accept it. For the most part, the extent of aid was to call out the National Guard and their equipment to help clear snow.

Some of the publicity the storm generated was in the national publication, "Look" magazine. In the aftermath of the storm, a local NP employee, Mel Diers was photographed shortly after the storm ended. The photo was of Mel repairing a telegraph line. What's so remarkable about that? The line he was repairing was hung on a cross member attached to a pole, with the cross member at least ten feet above ground level. He was sitting on snow, repairing the wire at eye level; the snow was that deep in the area of the wire break.

As we said earlier, we didn't have school Thursday and Friday. Days off because of storms didn't shorten our school term at all; we still had to go to school 180 days. But every time it snowed and the wind blew, we would set by the radio in the morning hoping for a storm day. I really don't know why, but we lived for them. Of course there was really nothing to do because we wouldn't want to go outside if it was storming. We just drove Mom crazy on storm days.

Steele was practically at the very center of the '66 blizzard and had it as bad as anyone. From Wednesday through Friday somewhere in the neighborhood of 28 inches of snow fell and there were wind gusts in the region clocked as high as 60 to 70 miles an hour that continued into Saturday. If you looked out any window in our house and tried to catch a glimpse of anything that was more than just a few feet away, all you could see was white. Visibility ranged from zero to 1/16th of a mile from early evening Wednesday until Saturday morning. The states of North and South Dakota and Minnesota were most affected by the storm and to a lessor extent Montana, Nebraska and Colorado.

This was the kind of storm where farmers have to tie one end of a rope around their waist and the other to the house when they went to the barn to check livestock. Farmyards were buried and herds of cows drifted for miles with the wind. They only stopped when they found good shelter; the snow got too deep or if they hit a fence that wasn't buried. One of my uncles actually gained cows during the storm. He was never able to find out who they belonged to. They probably drifted many miles with the wind. Up to twenty thousand head of cattle and sheep perished in North Dakota alone during this storm.

The storm also killed literally hundreds of thousands of pheasants, effectively destroying pheasant hunting for many years. About a month after the blizzard, I remember driving by a slough that had a pretty good willow patch in it. There were dead rabbits hanging in the willow branches about 8 or 10 feet off the ground. So the drifts were at least that deep in that slough.

Dad got a call during the storm that there was a fire in a trailer on the west edge of town. The trailer was the home of the young family of an employee of Wallin Motors. Their overworked furnace exploded and started a fire that, with the aid of the wind, very quickly engulfed the trailer. The family escaped unharmed, but because the fire spread so quickly, they escaped with just the clothes they were wearing, everything else burned. He had a brother in town who they stayed with until they got back on their feet. Luckily they lived in North Dakota. North Dakotans have not, and never will abandon a family in distress like that. Dad was the fire chief, and he and a couple other brave souls took the fire truck to the fire, arriving after a very tough journey just in time to see the trailer walls collapse and the fire almost out. It must have burned like it was in a blast furnace.

The storm caught a couple of Fort Yates high school coaches on their way back to Ft Yates from Mandan (a distance of about 65 miles). Drifting snow stopped their car and it eventually stalled, probably when drifting snow plugged the air intake or got the ignition wet. In their car, the coaches stayed warm burning wooden fence posts that they tore out of a fence on the other side of the highway ditch. They survived with only slight smoke inhalation problems.

The storm stalled and buried a passenger train, the "No. 1 Mainstreeter" on the Northern Pacific main line near New Salem, west of Bismarck, and temporarily trapped the passengers in the cars. On the Northern Pacific main line there are below ground level cuts in several areas that the trains have to run through. The storm quickly filled them with snow and it was that deep snow that stopped the trains. Then parts of the train were completely buried by drifting snow. The passengers (whose numbers included passengers from as far away as Massachusetts) were evacuated to New Salem where they were cared for by the residents of New Salem. There was another passenger train the "North Coast Unlimited" stalled 20 miles further west near Glen Ullin and sandwiched in between them was a freight train. Passenger and freight traffic by rail was disrupted for most of North Dakota for almost two weeks.

At one point late in the storm, Dad and I walked downtown to his store, mostly so we could check on the furnace. We went back into the shop. It had big doors at one end to move equipment in and out that was being worked on. The doors were probably 12-14 feet high. We opened the doors up and there was a wall of snow all the way to the top of the door opening. We left the door open for a while but closed it when the wall of snow started melting and collapsing.

Steele lost power early on Saturday morning, late in the storm, but it was off only a few hours. Power was restored when the local MDU service rep, Emil Hockhalter, along with a couple other Steele residents walked through the storm to a switching station on the northeast edge of town. There, Emil was able to reroute Steele's power so that they received it from lines to the south instead of the west. After the storm, he was thanked by the community for risking his life. Emil shrugged it off, he said he was just doing his job. Only in North Dakota!

The storm blew itself out on Saturday and the clearing of snow started almost immediately. When all was said and done, 18 deaths attributed to the storm were recorded in the Northern Plains states and in the same states, something like 130,000 head of livestock perished. When we got out of our house, all of Steele was truly a winter wonderland. On the main east-west street, we could walk on drifts that took you right up on top of buildings. There were cars completely buried under those drifts! With the storm over, the railroad brought out a huge engine mounted rotary snowblower and a snowplow that was also mounted on an engine to help dig the trains out. In New Salem and Glen Ullin they hired local people to shovel snow that was packed around the stalled passenger train cars and could only be moved by hand. There were huge drifts that completely blocked highways. It was amazing. A friend of mine related to me that his Dad had told him during the storm that this was the storm of his lifetime, and that he'd not see another like it. That was 40 years ago and his prediction has held true so far. We've seen nothing even remotely similar to it.

The uncle that gained cattle during the storm lived about 13 or 14 miles mostly south and a little west of Steele. Another uncle, who lived in town at Steele, was in the construction business and had a front-end loader nearby. He took the loader and headed south of Steele, and cleared the farm to market road, about 10 miles of pavement. He then cleared the other 3 or 4 miles to my uncle's farm. We drove down there that afternoon. The snowdrifts that my uncle dug through were incredible. Some cuts he made had sides that were at least 10-12 feet high.

Here in North Dakota we are exposed to the worst winter weather in the lower 48. Even though we know winter is coming by the calendar, the first snowfall of the season always makes front-page headlines in the local papers. You would think that the newspapers would take it a little more in stride. They were probably having a slow news day, heck; in North Dakota they almost always have a slow news day. The people of North Dakota do have a very healthy respect for Mother Nature.

That being said, one of the things that is a constant irritant to us is the meteorologists on the local TV stations that are constantly over forecasting the severity of winter weather systems. As much respect as we have for Ma Nature, sometimes common sense has to prevail. Here in North Dakota, we get what we call Alberta clippers several times a winter. A clipper is a low-pressure system that approaches our state out of the northwest, usually from Alberta. About seven times out of ten, the clippers are so starved for moisture that all that happens is we get a few snow flurries and a lot of wind. Historically if a clipper comes through and we get 3 or 4 inches of dry snow from it, that is about the absolute maximum amount of snow we could get from a clipper. Whenever we get a new weatherman at one the local TV stations or a new meteorologist at the weather service office, it takes them up to 2 or 3 years before they learn to not believe their computer models. The models always suggest we are going to get 4, 6, 8 or even more inches of snow from a clipper system. It just doesn't happen. They just need to talk to any longtime North Dakota resident and they'll set them straight. If you look out the window and nothing's happening, but the weatherman is forecasting –50 wind chills and lots of snow, and you have to be somewhere other than where you're currently at, you just hope for the best and prepare for the worst. You throw some Sterno, food, a sleeping bag, warm clothing and some winter boots (that's what we call a winter survival kit) in your vehicle and head out. We are cautious, and 95 times out of a 100 we'll get there. The other 5% of the time we give small town motels some business.

You will find that the average North Dakotan knows more about meteorology than people in any other part of the country. Nowhere else in America will you overhear a conversation that includes the words "pressure gradient" and "dew point" while you are walking through a shopping mall.

I'm pretty comfortable with cold weather, but to be honest there is at least one thing I don't like about the cold. That one thing is the fact that on rare occasions the temperature will hit 32F or below every month of the year. If you're a gardener you'll appreciate that more than a non-gardener. One summer we lost the potato patch to frost on the 4th of July. It wasn't at the farm, it was in a low-lying area north of town, but you've always got to be on guard. I have a friend who watched it snow west of Bismarck the same 4th of July.

When people talk about our state they say there are only two seasons in North Dakota, winter and bad ice fishing. As much as I would love to ice fish in the summer, you can't drive on the water in July like you can in January. Not with a pickup anyway, you've got to use a boat. There's a story that the Air

Force guys that guard and man the missile fields used to tell (and maybe they still do). The story goes that they stopped to talk to an old farmer one day. They asked him what he likes to do in the summer, to which the old fellow replied "Well if it falls on a Sunday, I usually go fishing".

You may not agree with this, but to a certain extent, cold is just a state of mind. Most, but not all, North Dakotans have the innate ability to adjust their bodies to changes in temperature. By that, I mean as it cools off in the fall, an outside temperature of 40 feels very cold, but on the other hand a temperature of 40 in January feels almost like picnic weather. So to a certain extent, cold IS just a state of mind.

So with weather like this why would I want to live in North Dakota? Its simple, the reason is what I've been implying all along; it's the people and the freedom. For instance, my dad used to leave the keys in the old pickup out in the farmyard, so that if there was an emergency and someone needed to use it, they could just hop in and go. We'd get it back later. Another freedom, just a different way of looking at it. That would only happen in the Dakota's. One other thing (sorry, this isn't about weather) about the people that everyone should be aware of. If you drove to town to work or shop in late summer or fall, you had to be very careful to lock your car or pickup doors while you were doing your business. If you screwed up and forgot, chances were better than 50-50 that your car would be full of zucchini, tomatoes or both when you came out to go home.

When I was in college, for a couple summers I crop sprayed to earn money to help pay my college bills. The summer after my freshman year, the spraying season had wound down, it was mid-July, and I had my crop sprayer, a Spray Coupe, in the backyard cleaning out the spray nozzles. While I was cleaning I noticed a threatening cloud coming out of the southwest. So, I started picking up the nozzles to take them in the garage because of the showers approaching. I had them all in my bucket and I leaned over to pick it up. All of a sudden the wind machine turned on and when I straightened up it almost knocked me down. Our family dog, Chipper, was out with me and I scooped her up and headed for the gate to get in the front yard and then behind the house out of the wind. Mom happened to be on the north side of the house where I was headed. She was painting. I got to the gate and the wind was blowing so hard, I couldn't get the gate open. Then suddenly it seemed to flip open and I got behind the house and put down the bucket and the dog. Mom hollered to me she didn't know where my little brother was. Twice I went around the corner to try and find him and got blown back. It turned out that my brothers were both in the house and Rob had thrown Darin in the closet when the storm started. Darin was madder than a wet hen at Rob for throwing him in the closet. He was only 5 years old and didn't understand that Rob was being careful. Just as quickly as the rain and wind had started, it quit. When we looked around there wasn't an undamaged tree in the yard. The reason the gate had suddenly opened so easy was because a tree had fallen on the fence, flipping the gate up in the air. Some how the tree had missed me. Have you ever heard the term microburst? That's what this storm was. A very sudden, very localized, incredible down burst of wind and rain. Not something you want to see too often! It took us weeks to clean up the mess, but we did have a heck of a bonfire.

One winter morning when I was home from college for a weekend or a holiday, I don't remember which; I went out to the barn for some reason. I noticed snow that was tracked inside the west door of the barn. That door is on the opposite side of the barn from the house. Curious, I went to the door and opened it. There in the previous nights new snowfall, was a set of tracks coming to the barn from the road. Those tracks also returned to the road. Now what would anyone come into our barn for in the middle of the night? So I looked around the barn a little. In a manger of one of the stalls, covered up with a little hay, I found a 12 pack of beer. Every kid in our house of course denied any knowledge of the beer, so we put it in the fridge and Dad and I drank it. I'm sure it belonged to brother Rob or sister Ruth, but they denied it. So the moral of this story is this, "Don't leave footprints in the snow when you're hiding your beer. If you do it will surely disappear". I'm sure you've used that one many times!

CHAPTER 7

SPORTS

The outdoor recreation complex at the Steele-Dawson high school was built in memory of Mark Abbott, who died in a car accident in the spring of 1974. Mark, who was a junior in high school, was a passenger in a car driven by a friend, Bruce, who also died in the crash. In a small town, tragedies like this affect the whole town. In Steele you knew everybody, some better than others, but at the least you said hi to whoever you met on the street. Mark was a great athlete whose best sport was football. Watching him play high school football was like watching a man play with boys. At 6-3 and somewhere in the neighborhood of 240 to 250 pounds he was pretty intimidating. He may have been the first kid from Steele or Steele-Dawson High School to play major college football. Whether he would have or not is certainly open to speculation, but he was that good.

He was a farm boy who developed his strength and stamina a little differently than most big time athletes. He did it the old fashioned way, not so much by lifting weights, but by hard work out on the farm. He had it all; just what the big football schools are looking for in a recruit. He was big, strong, fast and quick. He spent every summer and early fall working on his parent's farm as well as his Uncles turkey farm. When his uncle shipped his turkeys to market, every one of the many thousands on the farm had to be caught and crated up. That was Mark's and his brother Jeff's job, and that certainly helped Mark to develop his strength and agility.

His brother Jeff was also a good football player but he wasn't anywhere near as big as Mark. The talk around town was that Mark was already being recruited by Notre Dame and some other Division IA programs before he and his buddy died in that accident. Whether or not that was true, there is no way of knowing for certain.

Before my brother Rob severely injured himself in the spring of his sophomore year he was also an unusually good athlete. He was also fairly good sized and strong, but his greatest attribute was pure speed. If he would have finished high school uninjured I have no doubt he would have been recognized as the fastest kid in the state. Mark Abbott and Rob were both in the same class in school. When Rob was a sophomore wide receiver at Steele-Dawson he beat Jon Vetter, an exceptional defensive back from area football power Emmons Central for a 90-yard touchdown. He ran away from him. Vetter was a senior who the previous spring was the Class B State 110-meter hurdles champion. We pretty much always took a pounding in football from Emmons Central. The 90-yard touchdown pass that Rob hauled in had Steele-Dawson in the lead for most of the game. Unfortunately, they did lose that game 20-14 when Emmons Central scored in the last couple minutes.

That spring he sustained the injury that changed Rob from a phenomenal athlete to just a good one. He just couldn't catch a break. Rob was at the state track meet and was running the anchor leg in, I believe, the 4 X 200M relay. He took the baton and was accelerating when bang; he tore his pelvis apart. He managed to tear a strip of bone up to an inch wide off of his pelvic bone. A really terrible injury. I'm not sure you can even imagine how painful that was. It took a very long time to completely heal. It would have been a treat to have watched Mark Abbott and Rob play football their senior year if things would have been different. Their lives serve as a good example of how nothing is for certain in life and how quickly lives can change. It's also a good reason to never put off until tomorrow what can be done today. You never know what's going to happen tomorrow!

Okay sports fans, I hope you've studied, I've got a question for you. In what sport does North Dakota lay claim to the 2005 Junior Women's National Champions? No it's not basketball. No, it's not hockey. You give up? It's curling! I know, I know, I hear you saying since when do any of us care about curling? While curling is played in many North Dakota towns both large and small, I do know it's not necessarily a popular spectator sport here. I think it's fun to watch, but most others apparently do not share my opinion. Curling was a sport in the past Winter Olympiad and they did televise a fair amount of it, but most or all of the curling coverage was before 7 AM. It's too bad it couldn't have been shown at a better time, but we know television is all about ratings. If they show it, someone has to watch in order for advertisers to pay the bills. Anyway, congratulations young ladies! Now I'm going to tell you everything I know about curling, so pull up a chair and listen. As Boris Badanoff must have said to Rocky or Bullwinkle at one time or another, "You **vill** be interested".

Today, Canada is the center of the curling world. There are probably more curlers in Canada, particularly in eastern Canada, than the rest of the world combined. Their fondness for ice may have something to do with how few Canadians there are. They say that cold slows sperm activity, eh. Speaking of Canadian curling, during the last winter Olympics, they had a curler who was just absolutely amazing. His touch with those 42-pound rocks bordered on the unbelievable. Whatever incredible shot his skip (team captain) called on him to make, he executed it flawlessly. He was the reason why Canada won the gold medal.

Curling had its origins in Scotland in the 15th century. Leave it to the Scots to invent a game played with 42 pound pieces of granite. A few years ago the World Curling Championships were held in Bismarck. We attended some of the sessions. We were going to the Civic Center one evening and we just happened to walk from the parking lot to the arena behind a true Scotsman. He was big and tall, had red hair and a red beard, wore a kilt and tartan and spoke with such a strong Scottish brogue that I couldn't really understand him. He was a very imposing gentleman!

Curling is played on a 146 x 15-foot sheet of ice with 12-foot diameter targets painted in the ice on both ends. The teams consist of 4 members, each throwing two "rocks". A "rock" is that 42 pound piece of granite we talked about earlier, with a handle on top and a very smooth bottom. The object is to get more of your 42 pound rocks closer to the center of the target than your opponent does. So, it's actually very similar to the game of shuffleboard, but instead of the small disks they use the big rocks. I have also heard curling referred to as chess on ice, it can be a very cerebral game. When all players on both teams have thrown both of their rocks an end is completed, scores are calculated and all players move to the other end of the rink. A tournament game consists of ten ends.

The game is called curling because if you put a slight amount of clockwise or counterclockwise spin on the rock, you can curve or curl it. The guys and gals that are good at curling have an amazing touch to get their throws exactly where they want them, be it on the target or to knock an opponents rock off the target. It sounds boring, but it's very fun to watch. Incidentally, my daughter curls, she got started through friends and she enjoys it. There you have it, everything I know about curling. Go find a curling match somewhere next winter and watch, I guarantee you'll enjoy it.

When we were kids it seemed that all young boys were magnetically attracted to footballs and if more than three of us gathered together, a game broke out over at the local athletic field (Rev. Mertz/Knutson/Gilbertson/Benson's backyard). Football to most young men was almost a religion, something our parents never understood, because to most of them, the game was an unknown. Although football was actually fairly new in North Dakota, nationally, it was rapidly overtaking baseball as America's game. But, as much as we enjoyed playing football, baseball was still #1 in our hearts. In fact, baseball was still the reigning America's game in the late 50's and early 60's. In Steele, we had some great baseball players; we were just too good to shift gears to another sport.

When we got into junior high and started playing organized sports, the state said we had to have a "sports physical" every year. To be honest, I have nothing to compare my sports physical experiences with so I don't really know whether or not ours were typical. That being said, I have no doubt that some kids actually had more thorough physicals. In our community, our physicals consisted of taking your shirt and pants off. Dr. Z put his stethoscope on your back and chest and listened to your heart and lungs for a few seconds. He took a look down your throat. Then you were packed off to the bathroom to get him a urine specimen, which he held up to the light and quickly dumped in the toilet. The finish was to tell you to pull down your shorts, turn your head and cough, while he took a thorough look for a hernia. He would fill out your card, you would give him $5 and he sent you on your way. It certainly put our minds at rest. I guess the theory was "what you don't know can't hurt you". But to be honest, not one kid died in our high school while participating in a sport. Not one. Honest.

In junior and senior high in our small town America, sports occupied us year round. It was football in the fall, basketball in the winter and high school baseball in the spring and Legion baseball in the summer. You notice I didn't mention hockey, after all we're practically in Canada. All I can say is that hockey was unknown to us until we were about 12-14 years old and even then we didn't play hockey in any organized fashion. As close as we were to Canada, where hockey is the national religion, hockey was poor 4th or 5th when it came to choosing a sport in southern North Dakota. There was no organized hockey even in the bigger schools and towns in the western and southern parts of the state until a few years later. I guess, in the end, it boiled down to the fact that we all liked our noses unbroken and having most of our original teeth in our mouths.

From 1982 through 1996 Steele-Dawson High School had some excellent boys basketball teams. These young men and their coaches are legendary in Steele. Like we said a little earlier, when you get a winning program going, it seems like success breeds success. They all put in the time it takes to become winners. During that 15 year period, they made it to the State Class B tournament, I believe, 5 times. Before that run Steele or Steele-Dawson had never been in a state basketball tourney. While they never won it, they always showed that they belonged in the elite of Class B. The state tournament is an eight team affair and they play it all the way out to eighth place. I don't think they've ever finished below fifth or sixth.

Marty was one of those players. He went on to coach football at Carrington High School, where he elevated that program to one of the best Class B 11 man programs in North Dakota. His program produced a NFL player in Jim Kleinsasser, who is a tight end for the Minnesota Vikings. He currently has a player, offensive lineman Zach Harrington, in Division I college football at North Dakota State University. There is a story going around that when Kleinsasser was married a while ago in Hawaii, he wanted his old high school coach at his wedding. He flew Marty and his wife to Hawaii, at his expense, so they wouldn't miss the affair.

It's a sign of the times, but never the less very sad that of all the teams that we played in our district basketball tourneys, only about half are still playing. Our district consisted of Driscoll, Wing, Pettibone, Woodworth, Tuttle, Tappen, Steele and Medina. Of those schools, only Wing, Tappen, Medina and Steele still play and Wing is all but dead.

There is always a debate about whether it is coaching or pure talent that makes a team great. In Steele-Dawson, there is a good example of just how important coaching is. One of the coaches that was a part of that extraordinary run of boy's teams returned to coaching at the local high school, this time with the girls basketball program, when his daughters came of age. He is in his 4th year and two of his four teams, including the latest edition have gone to state. There you have it, the definitive answer (in this case)(sort of)!

A little earlier I promised you I would do some more bragging about Steele baseball, and here it is. In the sixties when I was a teenager, Steele was **the** baseball town. We had our moments in other sports, but in baseball we were always a force to be reckoned with. At that time, the American Legion program received an annual infusion of talented players from the Steele youth baseball program. We were on a roll at all levels of youth baseball all through the sixties. Also, we had very good coaching during those years, in particular John and Buzz, the Argent brothers. Yes they really did use Buzz as a nickname 50 years ago! We were well trained as well as dedicated and we loved the game

We started playing baseball at the age of 8 in the local Peewee program. I've got to admire people who coach at an entry level. Their patience and teaching capacity has to be almost endless. Then it was on to Babe Ruth and finally to Legion baseball. We typically played four years at each level. That wasn't a whole lot different than other small towns. The only difference was that we had learned to win and we expected to win. Sometimes we ran out of innings with us behind but it was a rare game that at least some good didn't come out of it.

When I was a Peewee we played our very first game at Medina (about 30 miles east of Steele). In my very first at bat in that very first game, I hit a home run. It wasn't over the fence, it was one of those inside the park types. I may not have been terribly gifted in many ways but I was fast. But, it's funny, the thing I remember most about that first game was splitting open the butt seam on my pants during the game. We only had uniform tops, so we wore jeans with them. Mom was able to find a pair of new jeans for me and I changed during the game.

When we got a few years older, we started bringing home the hardware in the Babe Ruth program. For a small town back then, there was no advancing to regional and national Babe Ruth tournaments, like they do today. Our tournaments covered a much smaller area. The area only extended from Tuttle to Napoleon (about 45-50 miles) north to south and Driscoll to Medina (about 40 miles) west to east. But we were kings of our small baseball world, a world where we won our league title in each of my last two Babe Ruth years. Those were just two of many that Steele Babe Ruthers claimed during the sixties.

As a result of our good training and also because we had an unusual number of very good ball players, we were the dominant Class B American Legion baseball team in North Dakota all through the decade of the 60's. During that era, it seemed that Steele, on an annual basis had one or two of the better players in the state. I know the team I was on had one of the best (I think he was the best) players in the state in my old neighbor Bill. Over about a 25 game schedule he hit nearly .600.

In 1962 playing in the state event in Cando, the Steele team, in the title game, lost a heartbreaker to Hillsboro. In 1965, the Steele American Legion team again finished second,

losing to Langdon in the state Class B final. In 1966 the
Legion team found themselves back in the title game again,
this time playing Velva for the state title. They came from
behind to win when Ron Blotsky hit a three-run triple in the
final inning. In 1967, the Legion team had another very good
year but lost a one run game in the region finals.

I started playing Legion baseball in 1968. We were state
tournament participants in 1968 and 1969, in New Rockford
and Mayville respectively. In 1970 I was part of the team that
beat Ellendale 13-8 up in Ray (near Williston) for the state
title.

In that state tournament, we had a stirring comeback in
our semifinal game against the defending champions, Hatton.
Hatton (near Grand Forks) is another traditional baseball
town. We were down 6-0 going into the sixth inning. We
loaded the bases and then a single and a double (by me) plated
four runs in the 6th. We completed our comeback in the
last inning (7th inning) when our best player and reformed
tricycle thief, Bill, hit a 3 run homer. The next day, late in
the championship game, Ellendale scored some runs to close
to within 10-8. Ellendale's catcher was very vocal that they
were going to get us. The next inning we got two guys on base
and our pitcher Gary hit a three run homer to put us up by
what turned out to be the final score, 13-8. I'll never forget
when Gary approached home plate he had a sneer on his face
directed toward the catcher that would have melted ice in the
middle of January. The catcher never said another word.

So, at that time, we had played in at least six of the last 9
state tournaments, we had played in four of the last nine title
games, winning the towns second title in 5 years. Steele won
their first and only other American Legion baseball title back
in 1933.

In 2004 the Steele-Dawson High School baseball team
finished second in the state to Cavalier, a town a little larger
than Steele in northeast North Dakota. That matched the best

showing in a high school athletic team event ever by a Steele-Dawson High School team. In 1965 Steele also finished second in the state in high school baseball, losing in the title game to Minot High something like 2-1. Those two finishes were the school's best, until this year, 2006.

Here is some history in the making. Steele-Dawson High School's baseball team finished the 2006 season 30-4 and defeated Langdon (not too far from Cavalier) 6-3 in the state championship game. This is Steele-Dawson High School's first state championship in any sport! Steele baseball was dominant when I was young and it seems it still is; Steele has been a baseball town for a long time. Several of this current group of high school players were also part of that Steele-Dawson team that finished second in 2004.

The four state titles in Legion and high school baseball are the only state titles in a team sport that Steele can claim. Steele and Steele-Dawson Legion and high school baseball teams have been in a baseball state championship game, I believe a total of eight times.

In high school baseball we played with the kids from Dawson, since it is Steele-Dawson High School. In the summer we split into two Legion teams and in our district, Dawson was our chief rival. Every year we had to beat them to get out of the district. That wasn't an easy task. There was a lot of baseball talent in the two towns.

During my senior year in high school, I was in Fargo making a campus visit to North Dakota State University (NDSU). I was in the dorm room that they assigned to me, when a shadow suddenly darkened the room. I looked up and there was a monster in the doorway telling me that he was my roommate for the night. Well, it really wasn't a monster; it was Sanford Qvale, a 6-8 and 300 lb. future NDSU offensive lineman. He was a young man from Ray, North Dakota. I went up to the field house with him and was quizzed by a couple of football coaches. One of them had been at a game

119

that I was playing in, but he had been there to watch someone else. He said he was impressed when I ran down the other teams tailback, a kid from Gackle, out of my middle linebacker spot. I was asked by them to walk on to the program. Standing next to Sandy, the big guy, I knew in my heart that I was out of my league, playing inside linebacker at 6'1" and 203 pounds. Our Legion baseball team's season was extended when we won the state Class B title and then were invited to the Class A state tournament. Because of that I didn't make the beginning of NDSU's fall football training camp. I was over a week late getting into fall camp. Within two weeks I had re-injured my left shoulder and also tore the meniscus in my left knee while tackling a 6-2, 230-lb. running back. That ended my less than glorious football career at NDSU.

I guess this is an example of what they mean when they say like father, like son. Sandy Qvale has two sons in Williston High School in 2005-06; one is a 6-8 freshman, built like his dad, and the other a skinny 6-11 junior. Talk about passing on your genes!

Before my alma mater (NDSU) moved up a level from NCAA Division II to Division IAA in football, the annual NDSU/UND (University of North Dakota) football game was a very big deal. At the time the UND/NDSU game was one of the oldest rivalries in college football with UND leading the series 61-45-3. Sadly, at least for the time being, UND won't play NDSU because of the division change. The game was played for the "Nickel Trophy" which of course was a giant "buffalo" nickel with a profile of a Native American (Sioux) on one side and the side view of a buffalo (Bison) on the other. The game was televised statewide if you couldn't make it to the game. It was the event of the year in North Dakota sports. Whole families would gather to watch the game. During the gatherings, it wasn't all that unusual to have fights break out between family members whose loyalties were divided. This was serious business!

One of the traditions surrounding the game was the theft of the nickel from the school that won it by someone from the other school. When my cousin's son, Corey, was a senior (I don't want to brag but he was also student body president) at NDSU, the nickel was in possession of UND. Corey and another NDSU student dressed as UND maintenance workers one day and walked into the building on the UND campus that housed the trophy. They had made coveralls to look like UND maintenance uniforms and in case they were challenged, they had printed up phony work orders. They just put the nickel in a toolbox and walked out with it! Then they sent the nickel on a US tour, taking pictures in front of landmarks all over the country. If it was stolen, tradition said the nickel was always returned before the day of the annual game.

CHAPTER 8

HOMES AND FAMILY

While I was in high school the family moved out to the farm where my parents still live, having lived there for almost 40 years. That meant no more combines and tractors parked out in the street. No more changing the engine in a truck overnight in the alley behind the house during harvest. No more trying to sneak in the house late at night and going up the squeaky stairs. We had lived in the old house in town more than 12 years. There our family grew from two kids to five. And there was only one bathroom! But that house with one bathroom had one more bathroom than the first house we lived in. At our first home, the bathroom was in a small house out in the yard. There were many from my generation that started the same way but I would bet that by the time we were 10 years old, civilization had caught up to all of us. Until at least the early 60's you didn't take it for granted that any given farm home had a bathroom. But progress was roaring into rural America, bringing electricity, indoor plumbing and television.

I don't remember a whole lot about the first house I lived in, other than my big sister and I slept in the same bedroom. I seem to remember there were only four rooms in the house, the bedrooms (there were two), the kitchen and the living room. You entered the house through the kitchen. From there you went into the living room. Both bedrooms were off the living room, kids to the right and parents to the left. It was a very small house.

When we lived in that first house, there were two Lennys in the neighborhood, my sister Lennis and our neighbors, Irma and Rex's youngest boy, Leonard. So when Mom or neighbor Irma hollered for Lenny, there would usually be two kids coming on the run.

Speaking of the first house (it was in Driscoll) I lived in, it was just across an alley from "Aunties" place. "Auntie" is the pet name we used for my Great Aunt Hazel. Lennis and I spent our day going over to visit "Auntie" and being dragged home by Mom. That happened at least a couple times a day. We loved visiting Auntie; she would give us coffee and cookies for mid morning and mid afternoon "coffee breaks". Of course the "coffee" was 90% milk.

To everyone in Driscoll my Aunt Hazel Nelson was "Big" Hazel. My Grandmother, also Hazel Nelson, was "Little" Hazel. Their nicknames had to do with their size, of course. Auntie was a pretty stout woman.

Auntie never married, lived in a tarpapered boxcar, never had indoor plumbing, drove a Nash Rambler, was a very good fiddle and piano player, loved to fish, was a pinochle fiend and knew everyone in town. She was quite a lady.

She made her living hauling mail sacks from the train depot to the post office and back the other way. In those days most mail traveled by rail, not by truck as it does today. I don't know how many passenger trains ran each day, but there were several. Each passenger train had a staffed mail car. The postal employees that staffed the mail cars were the postal service's elite. If the train wasn't scheduled to stop at a given station, the postal workers had a hook to snag mailbags that were hung on a pole alongside the track. Then they would just toss the incoming bag out the door as they were passing the station. If it was scheduled to stop they just picked up and dropped off. When they got the bag into the mail car, they would sort and rebag the mail. Aunt Hazel's job was to pick up the outgoing mail bag at the post office, haul it to the train depot and properly hang it on the pole. Then after the train passed, she found the incoming mailbag and hauled it to the post office. A pretty simple job, but someone had to do it.

Aunties' boxcar house was a simple but nice home. One thing we know for sure, it was cheap. It had no interior walls, so it was just a one-room house. It had been a refrigerated boxcar and so was well insulated, and because of that it was warm and cozy in cold weather. It was home to Auntie and she lived there for something like twenty years. The east-end was the kitchen with a table toward the center to eat on and serve as a pinochle-playing arena. The entry door was in the middle of the south side. The oil furnace was opposite the door and the combination bedroom/living room was on the west-end

One time, at band camp, (oops wrong story), when I was about 5 or 6 years old, Auntie took a couple of us kids fishing, I think it was at Crystal Springs. While we were there, some guys came with a big net and were netting fish. I think they must have been Game and Fish people, doing some test netting. One of the fish they netted was a rather large carp. I spotted it and told Auntie what I had seen. She talked me into going and asking the net guys if I could have the fish. They gave it to me (I remember that I couldn't figure out why they were laughing when they gave it to me) and I took it home. I don't remember what happened to that fish, but I'm sure it hit the garbage shortly after I arrived home.

I've done a lot of genealogical research on my family. The families of three of my grandparents are fairly recent immigrants. The earliest any of the three came to America was the early 1860's. But that research also showed that parts of my maternal grandmother's family have been in the United States since the early 1600's, well before the colonies were the

United States. I've also been able to follow that line back in Europe. There, in England, I've traced it back to the 1200's and the Plantagenet family of English royalty fame. Our ancestors in English royalty started at King Henry III and ended at King Edward I. There are just those two English kings in our ancestry. When I told my partners about my royal ancestors, they got all funny and started bowing and curtseying to me. All that formality is so silly; all they really have to do is just bow their head a little when they meet me in the hall or office.

Something interesting I found out while researching my family origins. Our family has an ancestor, Richard Lattin, who was married to my great, great, great, great, great Grandmother, Kezia Seeley. He fought with Ethan Allen and the Green Mountain boys in the American Revolution. He was one of a 175-man force that captured Fort Ticonderoga in the early days of the war. Also part of that force was the infamous turncoat, Benedict Arnold. Then mysteriously, Richard and Kezia moved to Canada after the war.

After we moved out to the farm, Rob had an owl that he kept in the hay storage area upstairs in our barn. An old rancher, Mark Holtz, had found a young flightless, whatever you call young flightless Great Horned Owls (owlets?), and brought it to him. The area that we kept it in was quite large, so he could fly around quite freely. We used to feed it live trapped mice from the granaries. We would turn them loose on the floor and the owl would bomb down off his perch and catch them. One day, a friend, Danny, was with us. We had a couple mice in a box and were carrying them upstairs in the barn. When we got up there, Rob accidentally dropped the box and a mouse escaped. Danny took off after it not remembering there was an owl on the premises. To make a short story shorter, the owl won a close race to catch the mouse, and in the process scared the wits out of Danny. A short time later, we released the owl. We hoped that we had adequately trained it. The owl didn't hang around very long. We don't know how it did in the wild, but, at the time, we thought if it weren't doing well it would have hung around looking for handouts. Its relatively quick disappearance meant that either it was somehow almost immediately killed or it was hunting okay on it's own. We chose to believe the latter

All kids grow up and of course those in our family were no exception. We started heading off to college, one at a time. Of the five of us, four graduated from a four-year college, (three from North Dakota State) with Bachelors degrees. Rob went to the Bottineau State School of Forestry, as it was known at the time. It was a junior college and he graduated from Bottineau with an Associate degree. With high school and college behind us, and our futures staring us in the face, we proceeded to scatter just a little. Three of the five of us ended up in North Dakota eventually landing in Steele, Fargo and Bismarck. The other two didn't wander too far, with one brother now living in Watertown, South Dakota and my oldest sister living and dying in Plentywood, Montana. Our youth was behind us and big changes were taking place. Our lives changed to include our college graduations, our weddings, our kids, new responsibilities, new jobs and careers and our own homes for our families. The farm changed from our home to the social center of our extended family. It also was the home, for several years, of the Spring Invitational National Croquet Championship. This was serious business and was held on Easter weekend every spring. It involved brothers, brothers in law, sisters, and sisters in law, etc., but was limited to anyone who could pick up a mallet. The croquet course changed from year to year and was always very interesting. We dispensed with the standard croquet wicket arrangement. Our course spread out over the farmyard, and involved snowdrifts, ditches, culverts, trucks, jumping our ball through the tire swing, roads and other obstacles. The only rules being that the wickets had to be set within the confines of the farmyard boundaries and participants could not be forced to go through water more than six inches deep. Did you know that croquet balls float? The prize for winning? You got to buy everyone a beer. If you get the feeling that we had a lot of fun playing the "Spring Invitational National", or as ESPN referred to it when they reported tournament results, the **"The Big Easter SIN"**, you would be absolutely right.

During this time we also held a family gambling outing over one extended Easter weekend. It was held at Prairie Knights casino south of Mandan. We piled into the van that brother in law John drove at the time and went to the casino. Do you know that if you are pushing someone in a wheelchair into the casino, they will come running and make sure they hold open the doors for you? Isn't that kind of them? They love to get your money! When we got into the casino, we proceeded to lose every cent we had brought along. There were no winners with the notable exception of the Standing Rock Sioux Tribe. When we walked out to the van and got in, one of us spotted a quarter and two nickels in an ashtray in the van. John immediately proclaimed it was a sign and we had to take the 35 cents in and parlay it into a small fortune. Didn't happen. We lost it in two spins of a slot machine. With that final blow to our egos, we limped home.

Also one extended Easter weekend we did something on Good Friday, something that was totally irresponsible, so much so that it will always be known in the annals of Stein history as **The Lost Good Friday.** The day started innocently enough. About mid-morning Rob and I decided to go gopher hunting. We decided to stop at Mark's parent's place. We wanted to see if Mark was there and if he wanted to go along. He was and he did. Then the day started to go to hell in a handcart. Mark brought along a 12 pack of beer. In the end, we were lucky we all survived. About noon we knew brother in law John would have arrived in town with his family, so we went to pick him up. Somewhere along the way we had picked up our hunting buddy, Kenny Mac. Of course, we needed more beer. In early afternoon we were on an abandoned farmstead north of Steele, checking the accuracy of some of our rifles. That's a great combination, firearms and beer. We found another abandoned farmstead that had copper lightning rods and copper ground cable still on the house. Of course we hated to see all that copper go to waste, so we 'salvaged' it to sell at a later date. Then we needed more beer. Mid-afternoon found us at a friend's place west of Steele. He took us for a ride in an old Buick Lasabre that had its roof cut off. We decided to see how fast we could go on the section line trails. Mark at one point tore off the sun visor on the passenger side and threw it away. The less I tell you about the day the better, so I won't talk a lot about a good portion of the day, although suffice it to say that at one point we thought we had killed Rob. I'll leave it at that; it was that kind of day. About seven or eight in the evening, since I was the responsible one (someone had to be), I figured I'd better get Rob and John home. When I did, they passed out in the living room, one in a chair and one on the couch. I went and got a beer. Now I'm writing about this only as a warning. Kids, don't do this! This is a perfect example of one of those cases where you need to do as I say, not as I do.

I don't know why we chose Easter weekend for these shenanigans. Probably because it was the one extended weekend where the family gathered together and the weather was usually nice. On the nice side of life, one of the longest running family traditions took place over that spring holiday weekend. That was the Annual Easter Egg Hunt. All the dads hid candy, eggs, and toys all over the farmyard on Easter Sunday and the kids searched for and found them. I think we did it for twenty or more years and finally ending with the last hunt taking place on Easter Sunday 2005.

Have you seen how the kids wear their caps sort of cocked off to the side and little off kilter and you want to reach out and straighten it out for them? My Dad started that. You all may just see him as an old farmer but he's a trend setter. Ask anyone in the family and they'll tell you. Whenever he was feeling really good or a little cocky about something, his cap would go a little to the side. My Dad, the trend setter. He didn't, however, start the wearing of caps backward. That was an idiot city kid thing.

When my little sister Ruth married her husband Gregg many years ago, they had a reception at the old community hall in Driscoll. My cousin Terry and his wife Sue were the host and hostess of the affair. There was free beer and champagne at the reception. It was getting fairly late and the free booze had pretty much petered out. The reception was turning into pretty much a family affair. Terry poured a glass of champagne for everyone and in the process emptied the last bottle. We drank and talked and sure enough the glasses dried up. Terry disappeared for a few minutes and reappeared with a fresh bottle. This happened a half dozen times. Terry apparently had hoarded a few bottles of the champagne for just this occasion. Thank goodness we have such a levelheaded conscientious cousin. Wait a minute, I didn't say that. He would be offended if he knew I had implied he was level headed and conscientious.

John recently bought a new pickup. He had gone to a dealership and negotiated a deal. After the negotiations were completed he told the salesman that "Aaah, I've got this van, see". He asked if he could get another $1500 knocked off the price of the new pickup if he gave them the van. They said they thought they could do that, but he should bring it in first. He brought it in, but when they saw it and drove it a little, they told him they were sorry but they couldn't give him $1500 for it. John told them that if they wouldn't give him the $1500, the deal was off, and he would take the van home. But the van wouldn't start so they had to assist him getting it started. When they got it started, he started to head for home.

Then they blinked. They waved him back and he got rid of the van for his price. If you knew how truly hailed out this van was, you would more clearly see the humor in this situation. Way to go brother!

John and my sister Lennis and their family lived for 12 years in Plentywood, Montana and now my sister is buried there. They moved to Plentywood from Miles City. Plentywood has to be one of the most isolated inhabited towns in the lower 48. Plentywood is about three or four times the size of Steele and because of its location, it still has a lot of businesses that not many small towns have. But, you have to want to go there. You just don't pass through there on your way to anywhere in the US. The only big city it is anywhere close to is Regina, Saskatchewan, which is about 150 miles north. Williston, North Dakota, population about 15,000 is about 80-85 miles south. As isolated as it is, John and Lennis' family has thrived there. Like I said earlier, beauty is in the eye of the beholder. All three of their girls were able to participate in a lot of extra curricular activities in high school, (actually, each of the 3 has claimed at least one state championship in sports, Sara in golf and Jill and Kristen in track) something they probably wouldn't have done much of in Miles City. I hate to say this, but the title of "Best Athlete in the Family" no longer belongs to one of us boys. John and Lennis' youngest daughter, my niece, Kristen is the best. It's not even close. I could talk about Kris all day long, I'm so proud of her. If you're ever in Plentywood, eat at Laurabelles, the owner is a Surrey, ND girl.

It is said that life always gives you a few lemons along with the sweet stuff. It is also said that if life gives you lemons you make lemonade. Our family got so many lemons that the lemonade we made from them is almost too sour to drink. Life has not been kind to my family. My mother is a colon cancer survivor; my dad's kidneys have failed, so he requires dialysis three times a week. I lost my older brother at the age of two to a congenital defect, called Biliary Atresia (no bile duct). I lost my big sister and John lost his wife in 2003 to pancreatic cancer. One of my younger brothers died from complications caused by MS. I have Parkinson's disease. I also recently had abdominal surgery to remove part of my colon that had a pre-cancerous mass in it. I do have one healthy sister and one healthy brother though. Fate has been a little hard on us, but you don't stop living if life gives you a lump of coal. You still get up every day and search for that diamond.

It looks like the Stein name in Steele may vanish in the next 20 years or so. There have been Steins in Steele for the last 95 years. I'm afraid that when my folks pass on that will be it. They and one niece are all that is left there, although to me Steele is still and will always remain home.

CHAPTER 9

MY LIFE

In the summer of 1982, when Gail and I and our young family had been in Bismarck about a year, we gathered with our new neighbors in one of their backyards on the Fourth of July for a picnic and a little celebration. It was about 8 in the evening everyone was about out of fireworks. Four or five of us guys, the neighborhood fathers, decided we would go to a fireworks stand and buy some more. Well, the operator of the stand we chose was anxious to close up, but did have some explosives left on his shelves. Apparently he felt he had made enough profit and was ready to deal. When we walked in, there were not any other customers, so he spotted us immediately and made us an offer. He picked up a fairly large box (about 18 x 24 x 18 or so) and asked us if he filled the box up with fireworks would we each gave him 20 bucks. We agreed and he started cleaning off his shelves actually putting hundreds and hundreds of dollars worth of fireworks in the box. The box was stacked as full of fireworks as he could get it. We took the box to our neighborhood celebration and we shot and shot fireworks until we were sick of it and we still had half of a box left. What a deal!

Until our 1981 move from Garrison to Bismarck, we had been preoccupied with starting our family, and other than our honeymoon in Manitoba and a trip or two to Montana, we were pretty much stuck in North Dakota. Part of the reason was economic, and also because our family was so young. That wouldn't change for a few more years.

However, when I went to work for a doctor group in Bismarck, **my** traveling habits changed dramatically. Most of my job at the beginning was taking care of clinical laboratory equipment for clients over a three-state area. At that time all of our trips were day trips, out in the morning and home by evening. Because of the distances involved to get to some client locations, on a lot of the trips we had to fly to cover the necessary ground. So, on one of my first days at work, we piled in a single engine airplane and away we went into the wild blue yonder! Of course, I had never been off the ground before except in a Ferris wheel and that's not quite the same. My education in single and twin engine plane travel was very quick, I had to fly, and I didn't have any time to work into it slowly. My lone work mate at that time, Bob, had recently obtained his pilot's license so he was able to fly on his own. I'm usually a pretty quick study, understanding new things quickly, so within a couple weeks I was actually copiloting a plane Bob rented. (He wasn't crazy enough to turn me loose completely, Bob was just taking a little nap.)

Over the years I suppose I accumulated in the thousands of hours of time in single and twin engine planes. Unlike a couple others in my office, I was very content to ride along, never cultivating much interest in becoming a pilot. But I could talk pilot talk with the best of them. ADF (Automatic Direction Finder), VFR (Visual Flight Rules), IFR (Instrument Flight Rules), flight plans, ILS (Instrument Landing System) approach, vectors, artificial horizon, compass heading, actual heading, GPS (Global Positioning System) approach, fuel pressure, flaps, fixed gear, retractable gear, Cessnas, Pipers, Moonies, ceilings, forward visibility, glide slope, downfield marker, final approach. I knew all the jargon. All those years of travel were quite a grind; but as a great man I know once told me, "It sure beat working for a living."

I also became a US traveler. My job included acquiring skills to take care of our client's equipment and since training courses are generally not available in Bismarck, I did a fair amount of traveling around the states. Trips were made to Dallas (multiple times), Beaumont (Texas), Atlanta, Miami, Boston (multiple times), New York City (Westchester), New Jersey and Chicago. It was quite an education in more ways than one. I was able to take Gail along a couple times, to Miami and Beaumont.

It wasn't too long after I started that our workload required another person, so Chuck came to work for us. Chuck and I went together on a training trip to New Jersey. It was unforgettable for more than one reason. On the flight from Minneapolis to Newark, seated very near us was a blonde, who was obviously a body builder and was carrying a golf club. When we arrived in Newark we called for a shuttle to our hotel. We had to wait outside. When we went to where we were supposed to wait, the blonde was also there. We huddled behind her until our shuttle arrived, just in case there was a mugger around.

This trip required more than a week, so we had a free weekend in of all places, Newark, New Jersey. So, on the weekend of the Jersey trip we took a bus into Manhattan in New York City. Once there, we went into the 42nd Street Port Authority terminal to catch a subway train to the World Trade Center. When we were passing through the 42nd Street terminal, there were a lot of panhandlers sitting along the walls, some of them with piles of coins they were counting. At one point a fight came boiling out of a doorway right out in front of us. Toto, we're not in Kansas any more! It was a strange new world!

Most of what you've heard about subways in New York is true. Vagrants seem to pretty much live in the subways and use various areas for bathrooms, something that becomes very apparent as soon as you go down the stairs into the tunnels. Well, we had decided what train we had to take to get to the World Trade Center. Chuck climbed on board the first or second train that arrived at that station (it wasn't the right one). I stood on the platform, saying "Chuck that's not our train" about four times, each time a little louder. In the end I had to grab him and pull him out of the car, he seemed determined that he was going to ride that one, a train that was headed for Long Island.

We finally got on the right train, and when we got down to the Trade Center, there was just a glass wall separating the dingy subway station from an upscale shopping area in the towers lower level. What a difference when you stepped through that door! In the towers themselves, we rode an elevator to the top and took a look around. It definitely was taller than the state capital building (the capital is 18 stories tall, the WTC was about a couple zillion stories, I think). Then our itinerary said it was on to Battery Park on the south end of Manhattan.

From the WTC we had decided we would walk down to Battery Park, and from there we would take the ferry out to Liberty Island. On the way to Battery Park we walked past hotels with doormen, interspersed with abandoned buildings and then just north of the park, we walked past the New York Athletic Club. They are the organization that annually awards the Heisman Trophy to the best college football player every year. When we got to Battery Park, we both chuckled a little. It was exactly like we've all seen in the movies. There were several street performers panhandling and there were guys walking around selling "genuine" Rolex watches for $5.99. The park rangers walked around with bullhorns, occasionally warning people that the watches weren't worth anything. People who didn't understand English still bought them.

When we got on the ferry we noticed we were two of the very few white English-speaking people on the boat. The people on that boat were literally from all over the world. It's amazing that all those different nationalities of people were headed out to Liberty Island to see the Statue of Liberty, the #1 symbol of freedom and of the United States. People may criticize Americans for any number of reasons (and we usually deserve it), but they still recognize us as the bastion of freedom on this planet. One bit of irony is that the statue was a gift from the people of France to the people of the United States. Currently, we don't have time for each other. We (Gail and I) were at a sales pitch recently, during which we were told that statistically the top three vacation destinations in the US for foreign and domestic tourists are the Statue of Liberty, Mt Rushmore and the Grand Canyon in that order. They are the three great wonders of America.

The times I was in Boston I was able to see quite a bit of the town. Boston has so much history it's just amazing. You can walk in the buildings where some of the greatest historical events took place. You can stand on the very spot where the "Boston Massacre" took place. You get kind of an eery feeling. All the history that you learned so long ago actually occurred right there. Samuel Adams and Paul Revere actually walked on those streets. The Quincy Market is a fun place to snoop around and also to eat in. It seemed like there was about any kind of food you could think of at the market.

I went on a tour while I was in Boston that took me to Lexington, Concord, Bunker Hill, Breeds Hill, the Old North Church and I also visited the USS Constitution (Old Ironsides). Everything is so close together, at least by modern standards. Speaking of close, in what they call "Old Boston" the streets are very narrow. I'm a very poor judge of distance, but it seemed like from building to building some of the streets are no more than 30 feet wide (including sidewalks). They are laid out to follow old cow paths, so they go at every angle imaginable and the blocks are very irregular.

Bob and I got lost in Old Boston one evening while driving a rental car and I think it took us a half an hour or 45 minutes to escape. While wandering around during our quest for freedom, we came around a corner and there was traffic backed up for almost a block. We sat there for a minute or two, and then we noticed that the driver in the car in front of us was waving us past him. He was in a taxi. Then we noticed the whole row of cars were taxis. We probably would have sat there for a long time. It was a block that the old town taxi's used as a taxi stand. We did feel a little stupid at that point. In the process of escaping we went by the Old North Church and the Boston Garden Arena, slowing down momentarily for each one so we could look a little as we went by.

In the Old Boston area there is also a pathway marked with colored lines and arrows on the sidewalks called the "Freedom Trail" that you can follow as a walking tour.

A couple times I rode on the MTA, or the Boston version of a subway. A lot of the routes were underground but a lot of the stations; especially the suburban ones were above ground. The previously mentioned tour I went on showed us the original run of the MTA. It was only about a block or two long, across part of the Boston Gardens, not the sports arena, but the park. Only being a block or so long was kind of comical. They must have been testing the equipment or something like that. I can't imagine actually sitting and waiting for the train to come back so you could ride a block.

When the kids were older, we went on family vacations every summer for about 5 or 6 years. They were probably the most enjoyable things we did as a family. Destinations of our trips were to Rapid City and the Black Hills a couple of times, and once each to Winnipeg, Manitoba, Glacier National Park and Yellowstone National Park. When we were at the summit in Glacier this was posted on a bulletin board at a trailhead for backpackers to read:

"**Notice**: When you are backpacking you should always carry pepper spray to deter grizzlies and also tie small bells on your backpack to warn grizzlies of your presence. **How to tell the difference between black bears and grizzly bears**: Visually, the grizzly has a pronounced hump on its front shoulders. The track of a grizzly may be as long as six inches while that of a black bear is probably half to two thirds that length. The scat of the black bear contains pits from berries and fur and small rodent bones. Grizzly scat usually contains small bells and smells like pepper spray." I swear that's the truth! Would I fib to you?

The Black Hills are a really good family vacation destination. There are a lot of things for families to do there. Our favorite activity in the Black Hills was the water park south of Rapid City. In Yellowstone Park it has to be the animals, the elk, buffalo and bears. In Winnipeg it was the horse races. When we went to Glacier we rented a motor home for the trip. Just traveling that way was fun!

There is a time in every young person's life when hanging out with your parents is not the thing to do. As the kids got older we became more adversaries instead of allies so they didn't want to travel with Mom and Dad any more. Then, at some point their parents magically again become acceptable companions. I'm not pointing a finger at any specific generation; I was the same way growing up. I don't know exactly when it happens, but at some point most parents change from dolts to trusted advisors or vice versa, sometimes almost overnight.

Several years ago, along with my sisters family, we went up into the Beartooth Pass (the pass you go over when driving from Red Lodge, Montana to Yellowstone Park) on Memorial Day weekend. There was still a fair amount of snow up there, especially in several long ravines or cuts. I was amazed by the number of people who strapped skis and boots on their backs and climbed to the top of those cuts. Then they would put their boots and skis on and ski down them. You had to admire their tenacity. I don't think there are a lot of people who would have put themselves through that for a couple minutes of mediocre skiing.

The same weekend we camped at the Woodbine Campground on the Stillwater River in the Nye area on the edge of Montana's Absorakee Mountains (it's in the area southwest of Billings). It was a beautiful weekend. We were camped on a creek and the snowmelt was pretty rapid because it was so nice. So the creek was running fast and high. When we got up in the morning (I think we stayed two nights) in a little eddy in the creek at our campsite there were 2 six packs of Olympia Beer that had washed away from an upstream campsite. We waited until noon for someone to come looking for it. When no one claimed it, we didn't want the beer to get old so John and I felt we had to consume it.

I read or heard somewhere that to drive a car or own a dog, you have to be licensed, but they'll let anyone become a parent. I've always considered myself to be no better than a mediocre parent. Now, after my child-rearing years have passed, I'm still not sure that I ever was any better than mediocre. When you become a parent, a parenting instruction book doesn't arrive at the same time in the mail. There isn't one included with the infant either. You pretty much make it up as you go along and hope to God that you've done the right things. A few years ago, my son was talking to my wife and I about a friend of his who was always in trouble. While talking about the friend, he said to us "of course, he didn't have the good parenting that I had." I was amazed that he felt that way. At least we must have done more right than wrong!

I guess that if I've learned anything about parenting, it's these basic things:

Not all battles are worth fighting. You need to pick your battles carefully, some just cause hard feelings and very little good comes out it for either parent or child.

Don't burn bridges just to make a point.

Never be afraid to admit you're wrong, becoming a parent doesn't make you omnipotent; you make mistakes the same as before you were a parent.

Finally, talking about just about anything goes a long way, because communication is a key.

Our daughter is a registered nurse and she works at the best hospital in Bismarck. She's about a three or four year veteran and is very good at her profession. She certainly enjoys her work. Jamie is the sports nut of the two kids. She owns her own home and is going to make a great companion for a lucky man when the time comes. She is just a wonderful daughter.

A couple years ago we drove out to Washington and visited our son in Seattle. We did all the touristy stuff and had a lot of fun. The one thing that absolutely floored me was when he took us out to his garage and showed us his word working shop and some of his work. He had most of the essential tools and his work was beautiful. Where he got the aptitude and the desire to do that, I have no idea! I can't even successfully pound in a nail. Not only that, I really don't have the desire to pick up a hammer. He is an amazing young man.

But then how could these young North Dakotans have turned out any different? Raised in the environment they were raised in gave them innate advantages in life that most young people in other parts of the country don't have. Both of our kids are self starters, by that I mean they decide and do things on their own, they don't need some one there to always tell them what to do. We always urged them to make their own decisions, but in the end it would seem that is something they are born with. It's certainly hard to teach.

CHAPTER 10

WINTER FUN

Ice Fishing

I do have a confession to make to everyone; I'm an ice-fishing junkie. First, I don't think an intervention is called for quite yet, I think admitting I'm a junkie is the first step back to recovery. So, just what is ice fishing? Here's the scoop. As the name ice fishing implies, it has something to do with ice. So we need some real cold weather in late fall or early winter to make that ice. As an ice fisherman I'd like to see the real cold come by mid-November. Well, actually it could come earlier, but that may curtail waterfowl hunting. What's a sportsman to do, waterfowl hunting or ice fishing? If it freezes up early we **have** to go ice fishing. If it doesn't freeze we **have** to go waterfowl hunting. Gee, that sounds like one of those win-win situations, doesn't it? But seriously, to make a lot of ice we are hoping for some calm nights with below zero weather. Before we can ice fish we need to cover the lakes with ice. Then, when you have a thick enough ice covering, (you need 3 or 4 inches to walk on and at least 12 inches to drive on) you can walk or drive out on the ice. There you drill a hole through the ice surface of the lake with what we call an ice auger, clear out the slush from the hole with the slush inhaler and fish with a hook, line and bobber through the hole. That's ice fishing. It actually should be called 'through the ice fishing', but that's too cumbersome. Ice fishing is easier.

Wait a minute, what's a slush inhaler? Just one of the tools of the trade, or as my wife calls them, the tools of ignorance. It's a device that you slip into the hole and with one swipe clears 90% of the slush you create when you drill the hole, out of the hole. Pretty handy!

I've ice fished on Lake Audubon north of Bismarck for over 30 years. It is a very big lake but we're pretty familiar with it. We don't head out on the ice until there is over a foot of ice on the lake. When it gets that thick, as long as you stay away from shore and clear of islands you won't break through. We've found that if you have problems, they almost always happen along mainland or island shorelines. There, occasionally there are springs that weaken ice or also pressure ridges that fold down instead of up and create pools of water that get a thin ice cover. You can break through that thin ice and sink into or get hung up in the pool, so you need to be careful there. Avoiding snowdrifts around spots where houses have been sitting is also a must. Sometimes the weight of the snow pushes water out on top of the ice through drilled holes that occasionally don't freeze shut under the snow and then slush areas are born. They are rare, but I've found them once or twice.

Most winters when ice thickness peaks in February you will see 25-30 inches of ice covering the lakes. I've seen as much as 50 inches of ice on Audubon in late winter. You could drive a tank on that much ice. In fact the winter when it hit 50 inches it was almost impossible to drill through. We put extensions on our augers and we could get through about 45 or 46 inches. We had to cut through the rest of the way with an old spoon-style hand auger.

If you are wondering how serious I really am about ice fishing, I usually get a mailing address on the lake in the winter. We have a Cross Country Courier delivery run set up to deliver food to the fish house and take fish to my land home. I have a long power cord run out on the lake from Totten Trail to charge batteries. Are you buying any of this? I hope not. I do enjoy it though!

But why is ice fishing so addictive? That's kind of like asking how do you describe the color blue to a blind person? There is no answer to either question that I can think of. It may be that it's just me. Maybe I was born with an extra gene, and I'm just a cold and ice loving freak of nature. Why else would anyone willingly freeze your fingers for just a fish? All I know is that there is something special to me about fishing through a hole in the ice surface of a lake. Most non-North Dakotans and a lot of native North Dakotans don't understand this. There's just something about that bobber going down or that tip up flag popping up that gets my juices flowing. It's probably a good thing that not everyone has the same attitude toward cold, bobbers and flags that I have. If they did it would get awful crowded out there.

We ice fish a lot in what are called fish houses. These vary a lot in their complexity. Some are portable and can be hauled around in back of a pickup. They usually consist of a tent on some kind of base. On the other hand some guys buy or build more permanent fish houses with little kitchens and bunks and literally spend a whole weekend or more than a day at a time in them. Mine is a little more modest but suffice it to say that you could buy a small car with what I've got into it! I also have a portable house that I use early in the year and when the weather is nice. Anyway, I'm an addict and these are just more "enablers".

I've spent a small fortune on various ice fishing "tools" like the slush inhaler, a Vexilar "fish-finder" flasher, an underwater camera and more. I've also spent the last 10 years searching for the perfect tip-up. For those of you that don't know what a tip-up is, it is a device that suspends bait in the water and when a fish hits the bait, it releases a flag to tell you a fish has hit the bait. I've come close but I'm not quite satisfied yet. The end result of my research is that I've got half a closet full of various kinds of tip-ups just gathering dust.

Back in the mid 70's, I had an ice fishing buddy, Terry, who really liked his beer. He has since left the state and I haven't fished with him for many years. But while he was here, one cold morning, I think it was around 10 or 12 degrees below zero, Terry and I went out on Lake Audubon. We got our holes drilled and our lines in the water at about 9 or 10 in the morning. So the next thing on Terry's agenda was to grab a couple beers, one of which he handed to me. So I opened mine up and took a drink and we're standing there and talking and a couple minutes after the first drink, I took another. My beer was frozen solid. It was then I decided it really wasn't beer drinking weather and I passed on the next round.

In the late 80's back in Steele, Rob and I were talking to an older fellow, Vic (this is Marlys' dad), who was a very good friend of ours. There is a small lake about 12-13 miles almost straight south of Steele named Pursian Lake. To my knowledge it had been fishless during our lifetime. While talking to Vic he told us that three or four years before, either he or someone he knew, I don't remember which, had dumped a pail full of live perch into Pursian Lake. Shortly before he talked to us, he had put a minnow trap into the lake and he had caught a bunch of small perch in the trap. He suggested that we go ice fishing on the lake to see if there were catchable perch there. So the next Saturday, Rob and I went down to try it. We fished a couple spots for 30-40 minutes each without a bite and we were beginning to think that Vic was pulling our leg. We thought we would try one more spot, then call it a day. So we moved the portable house to a third spot, cut some holes and dropped a bait down one of the holes. When the bobber hit the water it immediately went down. Over the next three or four hours, we caught about a hundred perch, kept fifty of which twenty five were 13 inches long or larger and the smallest of the fifty about 10 inches. The biggest perch we caught weighed over two pounds. That is one heckuva perch in anyone's book. An average larger perch in most lakes is about a 7 or 8 incher that are about 3 to a pound.

But, alas, those were the only good perch we caught on Pursian Lake. We went back again to fish a couple weeks later. We hadn't said a word to anyone about it but there must have been nearly a hundred fish houses on that little lake. It was just covered! They quickly cleaned out the perch.

About 4 or 5 years ago we got another tip from Vic, this one was a lake about five or six miles west of Steele. This was another good tip. The fishing wasn't as good as Pursian Lake but was much better than average. It is a much bigger lake than Pursian and so it has withstood the fishing pressure that inevitably occurred after our initial visit. It's only problem is that historically it was always just a shallow slough and the big wet of the early to mid 90's and the record snow of 1997 filled it up. It is now slowly reverting back to its original depth.

Another quick note, today (May, 2006) we said goodbye to Vic. He lived a grand life and passed away at the age of 93. Vaya con dios, old friend!

A couple years ago, I was doing a little early season ice fishing on New Johns Lake. I had drilled an extra hole and had the underwater camera in the water and near the bottom. I was watching the monitor inside my portable fish house and noticed it was starting to spin around on its own. When it was spun 180 degrees, the snout of a medium size muskie filled the screen. The big fish spent another minute or so spinning and examining the camera and then decided he didn't want to eat it and swam away. That was neat!

We've found an ice fishing spot on Lake Audubon that is almost super natural. It's just a 3 or 4 foot gradual hump on a flat and for the life of me, I don't understand why it is so good. We originally discovered it probably 30 or more years ago. We have probably fished it over a hundred times over the years and probably caught as many as 2000 walleyes and perch (and most likely more) there. I think that much consistency makes it more than a fluke. We move on to the spot in late winter and the fish are almost always there. The GPS coordinates to get there are a closely guarded family secret kept in a mayonnaise jar on Funk and Wagnall's porch. That was a joke, they're just written on a map in my tackle box (but they are a family secret).

My little brother, Darin, lives in Watertown, SD. We used to go down every winter to ice fish on the lakes in that area. One of the lakes we have fished many times went by the interesting name of Enemy Swim. That's obviously the name that Native Americans gave it. As to your question of why, I have no idea. The first time we fished it, there was a lot of snow on the ice and we couldn't get around very well. We went as far as we could go which wasn't too far, set up the portable fish house and fished most of the afternoon. We caught quite a few perch, a few of which were cleanable. It was nearing sunset and we were hoping for a couple walleyes. We didn't get any, but I noticed that on the Vexilar we were marking fish suspended about six feet from the bottom. I lifted my minnow up that six feet and immediately caught a fish. When I landed it, I saw I had caught a crappie. The first crappie I had ever caught through the ice. There just aren't that many opportunities to do that in North Dakota. We both lifted our baits up and we caught about a dozen pounder crappies before they left us. We've been back 3 or 4 times trying to find them again but we haven't been able to repeat.

If there is one thing I've learned about ice fishing, it's that nothing is for sure. About the time you guarantee good fishing to someone, that's about the time the fish quit biting. I'm about as good as it gets on Lake Audubon, but I've learned the hard way that there are times you can't catch fish to save your soul.

There just has to be a best time ice fishing, ever, doesn't there? This winter (2006-07) I got on one of my traditional spots on Lake Audubon and had the best day ice fishing that I've ever had, and that's saying a mouthful. I fished from about 1 PM to 6 PM and I don't think I ever had more than 5 minutes between bites. I don't want to get into the boring details of what I caught, but I threw a lot of fish back. It was one of those special days that we all wish for, and this was a wish come true!

Snow Skiing

One of the great things about North Dakota, is its proximity to Montana and good skiing. North Dakota has tried to create ski areas, but has had a difficult time keeping them going, because of, believe it or not, lack of snow. Of course, there is also a marked lack of mountains here. In fact, there used to be a billboard along the interstate proclaiming that you were "Entering North Dakota, Mountain Removal Project Complete". (The billboard is real, but they really didn't have a mountain removal project.) At one time there was another billboard that read "Entering North Dakota, Custer Was Alive When He Left Here".

Until recently, snow skiing has been a passion of mine. I suppose you could say it still is but because of a long term less than beneficial relationship with Parkinson's disease, my balance is no longer good enough to comfortably ski. If at some point in the future a cure or at least improved treatment for my problem is available, one of the first things I'll do is get back into it. Skiing is a lot of fun, but beyond that, it is also a great way spend quality time with friends and family. Not being able to ski certainly takes away from my love of winter. Ice fishing is my remaining winter passion and it will have to do for the time being. Being an ice fishing fool helps, as you've already noted.

I guess I miss going skiing as much as I miss skiing. Hanging out with colleagues, friends and family with nothing more serious to worry about than which runs you're going on and where you're eating dinner that night. That is truly the life. But you know what they say, when one door closes, another opens up, if I could just find it. Could you help me look for it?

I don't think I've ever participated in another sport that gives you such a total body workout. After you've skied hard for 2 or3 days, I swear you can feel it in every muscle in your body, including some you never suspected were there. If I could ski more than a half dozen days a winter, I maybe could get back in something resembling good condition! On the down side spending those days active and in the outdoors, I always ate like I was starving to death. So if I were able to ski more, after a month of skiing I would be a well-conditioned blimp.

I wish I could have skied as a youth. I'm really envious of the young people who grow up near a good ski area. I would have loved to have grown up in Bozeman or Red Lodge, Montana. I love to listen to the kids while riding up on a chair lift early in the morning just after the lifts open. You can hear the kids laughing and hollering all around you. They sound like they're having the time of their lives. To be able to do that every weekend or at least most weekends is hard for me to imagine. I hope they realize and appreciate how good they have it.

So where do we hang out when we ski? I'm not terribly adventurous; my skiing experience has all been accumulated in south central Montana. All of my skiing has been at one of the southern Montana big three, Big Sky, Bridger Bowl, or Red Lodge Mountain. They each have special attractions for me. Big Sky has the most terrain and so has the best skiing, but alas, it is by far the most expensive. It is located about an hour southwest of Bozeman. It is the farthest of the three. Red

Lodge Mountain is the closest to Bismarck, and is the smallest of the three. We really like Red Lodge; it is the "homiest" of the bunch. Red Lodge has always had a problem with natural snow. Many years it doesn't get hardly any early in the skiing season. So sadly, although they make a lot of snow, you just can't rely on Red Lodge for good skiing. That leaves us with Bridger Bowl, located about a half-hour north of Bozeman. But, if you've got to settle for a ski resort, Bridger Bowl is a great alternative and we've spent a lot of time there over the years. It is big enough that you can do a lot of skiing without seeing the same stuff too often but at the same time a lift ticket costs about 50 to 60% of what a Big Sky ticket costs.

It's easy to see why the US had a lot of success in the snowboard events of the 2006 Olympics. I've seen many young people over the years I've skied who are just amazing snowboarders, especially at Bridger. There are a lot of them and they get better all the time. The Montana resorts are just getting themselves equipped for all the usual competitive snowboard events. Check back in a few more years, they can only get better. I've talked to several older people (30 or older) who have tried snowboarding and some who snowboard regularly and they all say that it isn't that easy, it requires more skill than skiing. It raises my admiration level even higher.

When I skied a lot, the focal point of every trip was to make that one "perfect" run down a hill. As the years went on my quest for my "perfect" run took place on more and more difficult terrain. If I made that one perfect run, I felt that I was progressing as a skier. Eventually I felt I was skiing about as well as I possibly could. I still continued my quest for that one "perfect" run each trip. Usually I got it somewhere near the end of the trip. Each "perfect" run was burned in my memory and fueled my desire to go back and do it again. My definition of a "perfect" run is one where I felt I'd skied my very best and there were no obvious slips or mistakes.

If you have skied, you know what moguls are (I hope I'm spelling it right). If you haven't skied, they are closely spaced mounds of hard packed snow that develop naturally on ski runs that aren't routinely groomed (smoothed out). They are very challenging to ski through, but some people learn to go through them quite quickly and even seem to enjoy it. They have an Olympic event where they ski through a 400-meter long mogul field and make a couple jumps and the Olympians run that course, all in something like 21 or 22 seconds. To be honest I could probably navigate the same course in something like an hour and a half. Those guys and gals are amazing!

If I were to choose one run at the resorts that I frequented as a favorite, that would actually be pretty easy, it would have to be Paradise at Red Lodge Mountain. It is just a lot of fun. As you read this you will see that I talk about Paradise a little later. You'll see that this run is special to me for another reason, one that you would never guess.

Big Sky

I learned to ski at the Big Sky ski area. One day, out of the blue, Dr. B, one of my former bosses invited Bob and me to come along skiing with him. He told us we would fly out in his plane and stay at his condo in the "meadow" below the resort. I was about 35 or so, a little late in life to learn, but better late than never. I packed up what little winter clothing I had that could be used for skiing. Gail found a pair of ski pants for me and with hardly any trepidation at all, I stepped off into the unknown. The first morning was lesson time of course but first, that morning I had to listen to an hour or two of verbal instructions from Dr B, none of which I understood at all. He was using slang and technical terminology and could have just as well been talking to me in French. I would like to say I was a natural, but that really wouldn't be true. I struggled mightily all morning and it wasn't until the last 15 minutes or so that the lights started to come on. So with the lesson done and after we had a bit of lunch, I headed up on the mountain with Dr. B and Bob. I was able to get off the lifts okay and that was about the only thing I could do. I spent as much time flying through the air as I spent on the ground. I was wringing wet all afternoon; I was working so hard. The next morning is when I learned to ski. I took an 'on the mountain' lesson with one of Big Sky's famous Austrian instructors. I think his name was Hans or Frans or something like that. After that lesson and before our scheduled quitting time, I went on a couple of Green (Beginner) runs, by myself, and I'll have to admit it was fun. Noon was quitting time for all of us and as we flew back to Bismarck I was feeling anxious to get back out again, but it would have to wait until the next winter.

I'm not sure it if was the next winter but I know it wasn't more than a couple of winters later, I went skiing with Dr. B again, this time with work mates Chuck and Marj. When we flew out this trip we parked our small twin engine Cessna right beside a corporate jet with the identifier of TJ1 on its tail. Of course that was Ted Turner and Jane Fonda's ride out to Bozeman. One of the evenings we were there Chuck, Marj, and I spent a little time in the hot tub. I noticed when I went out to the tub that right outside the condo door it was really slippery. It was fairly dark out there and so the slippery area was hard to see. Chuck and I were in the tub and Marj was late as usual. Finally the door opened and I started saying "Marj, watch out the" KABOOM! Marj had come running out the door, slipped, her feet flew up in the air, and she slammed down on her back. She felt that in the morning.

The same trip Chuck and I were skiing together. It was just a few minutes until the lifts closed down for the day. We saw a sign that pointed to a trail to one side that read "Bozeman Trail". We stood and read the sign and I must have said something about how I'd never been on it. Chuck said "How bad could it be"? So we headed for the Bozeman Trail. Chuck was in the lead, it was twilight, light conditions were poor, what we call flat light. It is very hard to see terrain in flat light. I was going along and looked out in front of me and didn't see Chuck. I made a turn and looked again and there he was. I thought to myself I just must have not looked over the whole width of the run and missed him. I was cruising along and the bottom dropped out from under me with no warning. I dropped into a ravine about 8 feet deep. When I hit the bottom my knees slammed up into my chest and then bang I was going up and popped out of it. In the flat light I hadn't seen it coming, it scared the heck out of me. Chuck must have been down in the ravine when I didn't see him. Then we hit the Bozeman Trail. It was a cross-country ski trail down to the condos. We thought we could take our skis off and walk, but when we tried that we immediately started sinking. We found the only way we were going to get down the trail was to keep our skis on and pole. We were sweating like butchers when we got back to the lodge. How bad can it be?

I've always had fun skiing at Big Sky and there are rarely lift lines, but you do pay for the solitude. It wasn't too long after I learned to ski that one of us in the office spotted an ad for a $99.00 ski vacation in a local paper. For that fee we would get three nights lodging and four lift tickets, both right at Big Sky. All we had to do was attend a 45-minute time share presentation. We called and found that they had three openings left for the weekend we wanted to go, so we took all three. So Big Sky here we come.

The guy that gave us our time share sales pitch tried his best to make us feel guilty for accepting the cheap ski vacation, but we resisted. If you are a real traveler time-shares will work for you, but we didn't feel we were in the right crowd.

It was during this trip that we discovered the runs on what is called the backside of Andesite. We didn't actually discover them, they knew they were there all the time. You know what I mean! Andesite is the name of the original ridge or mountain that Big Sky Resort started with. We found that the backside runs were fun and hardly used at all. It was on these runs that I had a couple of memorable garage sales. For those of you unfamiliar with technical skiing talk, a garage or yard sale is a fall, during which you lose practically everything except your shorts and socks. The first sale, I had just made it through the most difficult part of the run and had relaxed and was cruising when BAM, I hit an unexpected ridge in the snow and went rear end over teakettle and spread skiing gear over a fifty foot area. I had just barely come to a stop when about a seventy plus year old lady came skiing up and asked me if I was okay. Embarrassed, I said yes. The second sale I was skiing along, heard a faint click, realized one of my skis had just left me and then a moment or so later I held garage sale #2. There was a lesson to be learned from that second fall, always clean the snow off your boots before you step into the boot release on the ski.

One of the most famous runs at Big Sky is Mr. K, a long (I think 3 miles, but it could be slightly more or less) green or beginner run. You've always got to cruise Mr. K a few times when you're at Big Sky.

We met a young lady on that trip I'll never forget. She was quite young, probably 10 or 12 years old. She rode up in a gondola with us. We asked her what was the toughest run that she had skied. She told us she had skied off the Challenger lift (the most difficult terrain at Big Sky at the time) with her uncle. She had a wry smile on her face and a pin on her jacket that said "No Guts, No Glory". Today, she probably owns her own company. Heck, she probably owns several companies; she was a very confident young lady.

Bridger

Back when I worked for the doctor group, our business manager at the time (and future partner), Rosemary organized a company wide ski trip. Our bosses rented a bus and everyone who wanted to come along piled on after work on a Thursday.

We skied for two days and rode back on Sunday. Gail and I went along on two of the three trips they organized, going twice to Bridger Bowl, north of Bozeman, Montana. The second trip we went on, the bus had television monitors fed by a VCR. The first trip was tough; we had to entertain ourselves. On that trip, my future partner Chuck (who learned to handle dice in the bar in Willow City, I'm sure) was shaking dice with a cytologist's husband Dave and a cytologist Monica and a couple others and practically financed his whole trip. Future partner Rosemary and I took on all comers in hearts, but regretfully we didn't play for money. We were kicking butt and taking names. The bus rides in general were a lot of fun, **except** for one of the trips home. It was the day the bus' generator failed. Now you say why is that so bad. It meant no VCR, no bathroom exhaust fans, and when it got dark failing headlights. Also the fuel pump was electric. It was still working when he dropped us off in Bismarck, but the driver made it only another two or three blocks and it quit. That was cutting it close. The worst thing while we were going down the highway was the lack of a bathroom exhaust fan. Imagine three days of waste in the holding tank. It was a little grim. Of course it was a Sunday, so it was impossible to get it repaired. We stopped in Custer, Montana to check it out ourselves. There we met the Custer volunteer fire department out burning ditches. They were a funny bunch of guys. They certainly made the trip shorter by distracting us from our troubles for a while.

On one of the company trips to Bridger, it was nearing lunchtime on the slopes and a few of us were gathering for a break. My buddy Paul had talked to his wife before he came in and she told him she was going up on the Pierre's Knob lift with two or three other ladies. We took our time, because, after all, we were on vacation. We were seated looking out a window keeping an eye out for the ladies coming down from the knob. We figured we must have missed them because we were sitting there for almost 45 minutes. When we finished, we split up and headed out with Paul starting up to Pierre's Knob to check on the ladies. He hopped on the lift and skied over to the top of Thunder Road (a difficult intermediate run) and there stood his wife and the other ladies. They had been standing looking down the run for 45 minutes. She motioned him over to her and she tersely told him "Find an easier way down" to which he replied that he didn't know an easier way. She fired back, "I said, **find an easier way down**". So he did.

The Pierre's Knob lift itself is a thing of beauty. There is a point about half to two-thirds of the way up; it goes "vertical", or almost straight up and down. It is one of the most intimidating rides not in a carnival. When you dismount, if you turn left, you take a winding catwalk to the top of a blue (intermediate) run, Thunder Road. If you turn right very quickly you come to "Emil's Mile", the steepest blue (intermediate) run that I know of. One day Bob and I were standing at the top of Thunder Road about to take off, when we heard a commotion behind us. We looked up and back and two skiers came off the mound behind us, flew right over our heads and were gone. That was spectacular!

In my limited experience, I found there was only one way to handle intimidating runs. Like the Big Sky girl's pin said it is the "no guts no glory" way. When I was at my best, if I had never gone down a particular run, when I got to the top of that run, no matter how steep it was, I never hesitated and immediately went over the edge. I've often found that if you hesitate you often times talk yourself out of going. I found that becoming a good skier is as much a matter of overcoming mental obstacles as it is overcoming physical obstacles.

On several of our ski trips we went along with two other couples, partner Bob and his wife Lois and computer programmer Paul and his wife Lisa. They are great people and great friends. On this particular trip, the condo we were spending the weekend in had an outdoor hot tub. We were going to jump in the hot tub shortly after we got to the condo. Bob was lifting the cover off it while I was turning on the circulator pump. The pump fired up just as Bob had pulled off the cover and was leaning over the tub. Unknown to us it had leaked a large part of its water out onto the ground below it. Because of that it wasn't circulating water through its water heater. It could however still spray water out of the circulating nozzles. Imagine it's only about 20-25 degrees outside, with Bob in shorts prepared to get in the hot tub, leaning over the tub and getting caught full bore in a 35-degree spray of water. He was out of there even before his scream reached my ears. We were able to use the tub later when the caretaker plugged the leak.

When we had left Bismarck earlier that day, Paul didn't feel good, but he thought he would get better, which turned out to be only his dreams. He spent most of that ski trip in bed. I think he ventured out twice for a run or two each time but then retreated to his bed up in the loft. Paul had a miserable trip.

Paul's sick trip was probably the coldest ski trip I've ever been on. The ladies didn't ski all that much because of the cold. The first morning it was a few degrees below zero. Bob and I were two of the few that braved the cold. There was about 5 inches of fresh powder that morning also. Now I wasn't very experienced skiing in powder and one of the first runs we were on, I caught a couple of ruts, did the splits and ended up doing a face plant (skiing talk that means you fell face first). I was okay; I'm a cold weather freak. It doesn't bother me. However when we reached the lift station, a concerned attendant wanted to get me to go in the lodge and take a break. I guess me looking like a snowman might have made him think I was in trouble.

One of the neatest places we've ever stayed on a ski trip is a bed and breakfast northeast of Bozeman with the name The Howlers. I've been a big critic of the US Fish and Wildlife

Services (or whoever is responsible for this tragedy) plan to re-establish wolves in the wild in the northern Rockies, so it's clear I'm not a big wolf fan. If I get started I can go on all day on that subject. But this place is really neat. The first night we stayed there we went down to the B&B's recreation area on the lowest level and when we walked in there appeared to be framed life size photos of wolves on one of the walls. I didn't realize until several minutes later that the "framed" photos on the wall were actually real wolves sitting or standing outside and watching us as we moved around inside. What a kick. The couple that owns the place moved to Bozeman from Hawaii, another of the west coast types that have fled the coast and moved to the northern Rockies. The husband of the couple was a body builder. When we were in the recreation area, all of his weights were available for use by the guests. He had 130 pound weights for doing one arm curls! I'm not a 98-pound weakling and have done a lot of weight lifting in my day, but I couldn't even pick up one of those weights with one hand. One of the days we were skiing was Valentines Day. I had talked to them before we went out there about bringing in some flowers on Valentines Day while we were out skiing. So, when we returned from skiing there was a pretty bouquet of flowers and a box of candy for the ladies from us guys. It turned out to be the hit of the trip. It was a great place to stay, and I highly recommend it.

A few years ago we were at Bridger Bowl when they held the NCAA National Collegiate Skiing Championships there. There were a bunch of good skiers there, some all the way from the east coast. It was a lot of fun to watch. One thing that amazed me was that the teams used the lodge's cafeteria as a locker room. It was almost enough to make me quit skiing and hang around the cafeteria. There were many very attractive young ladies on those teams. Need I say more?

I have to make a comment on what we think is the most beautiful spot in any of the Montana resorts. There are actually a lot of great views, but this is what I consider the best. If you take the Alpine lift at Bridger Bowl to the top then take a right and ski down the trail until you pop out of the trees at what they call North Meadows then ski to the top of the first rise. Just stand there and look out in front of you. It's breathtaking. There is a bit of philosophy that applies to moments like this. It goes like this: "Life isn't measured by the breaths we take but by the moments that leave us breathless". This will leave you breathless.

Once while skiing with my esteemed colleague, Bob, at Bridger, we went up a short lift called the Deer Park lift. I knew that the only run down off that lift was quite steep. I actually think the lift is there only for competitions where they need steep slalom courses. When Bob and I reached the top and cleared the shack, as soon as I heard my ski's chattering I thought, "Oh great, it's icy. If you are an experienced skier, you learn to recognize the chattering sound your skis make when going over ice. So, I was on a steep run, an icy steep run. Also if you're an experienced skier you immediately know that on ice, you really need to control your speed, so you keep yourself slowed down by turning more and you make it just fine. As I was coming down, about half way down the run, another skier who fell somewhere behind me slid almost all the way to the bottom, passing me in the process. We didn't go back up, there were other runs that were more fun that day.

At Bridger Bowl, the Alpine lift goes over a deep little creek bed that over the years has gotten skied by us dozens of times and has been named semi-affectionately by us the "little creek of horrors" Once you've skied down into it you're stuck and you've got to ski it out to the end. Most times it's not that bad unless there's a lot of fresh snow. Then it tends to make you work to get out. More often than not we've had a lot of fun in that "little creek of horrors".

Probably the single best skier I've had the pleasure of skiing with is the son of my partner Bob. The young man's name is

Scott. He is also a friend of mine; I've known him his whole life. He is now thirtyish, married and the father of three. He is the only person I've seen go into the creek at Bridger and come back out at the top. He skied in at full speed went right through the bottom, up the wall at the top of the creek, came out flying through the air and came quickly to a stop right beside me. Pretty darn good Scott! The few times we have skied together, Scott has done his best to lure me into areas where I know I shouldn't be. He doesn't realize that living as long as I have only sharpens your survival instincts.

Red Lodge

We've skied at Red Lodge at least a dozen times over the years. Red Lodge is the smallest of the southern Montana Big 3, and it has the homiest feel. The town of Red Lodge is just big enough, but not too big. It's just a nice place. The ski area is small enough that when they start grilling hamburgers before noon on a fairly calm day, the smell permeates the area between the base lodge and the mid mountain lodge. It pretty much clears the lower slopes. Talk about a dinner bell!

I wasn't a black diamond or expert slope skier, although I occasionally would try them out. I have gone down (in a fashion) one run at Red Lodge that is steeper than anything I've ever skied on in any of the ski areas. I have a method to judge the steepness of a slope. If you can stand sideways to the slope and reach out and touch the snow beside you without having to lean or bend at all it is one steep mother. On one of our visits to Red Lodge I stood below and looked up on a short run by the name of Pine Ridge. From the bottom it looked steep, but how bad could it be? So I went up on a lift to get above it and got myself to the top of the run. Now standing on top and looking down, wow, this mother was steep! Using my method, you didn't even have to stretch your arm out to touch snow. It was so steep; I couldn't see the bottom of the run. Anyway, I went for it, actually made it about two thirds of the way down, fell and slid the rest of the way, much to the delight of the people riding the chair lift directly above it. They love watching you get dumped.

Several winters ago, we were in a condo on the golf course at Red Lodge ready for a weekend of skiing. However the local forecast was for very cold weather. We woke up the next morning and the thermometer read −18. I'm a cold weather freak, but that's a little too much. We called up to the resort and asked what the temperature was and they told us +15 or some where in that neighborhood. We thought sure, anything to get us up there. We got dressed anyway, grabbed our gear and headed up the mountain. We were checking the temperature on the thermometer in the vehicle on the way up and it was -15, -16, -17. We pulled into the lower parking lot and it was still −17. We continued up and around the corner maybe 30 feet or less higher elevation and lo and behold the temperature rose from −17 to +15. So we went skiing, it was amazing.

At Red Lodge the main chair that feeds up from the base lodge is a triple chair, or one that carries three people per chair. One day myself, my good friend Lois, and another mutual friend were riding up on the triple. Lois has many talents and one of them is talking. She was talking away to both of us all the way up and we were nearing the dismount station. Jack and I had lifted up the tips of our skis as you are supposed to, not really paying attention to Lois, who was still talking and suddenly before we reached the dismount surface, Lois quit talking. Both Jack and I glanced over at the same time and Lois had disappeared. She had forgotten to lift up her ski tips and they caught in the catch net just before the shack and she was jerked out of the chair onto the net. Luckily she didn't get physically hurt, only her ego was bruised.

My buddy Paul's daughter was skiing with us on Lazy M, a long Blue (intermediate) that is what could be called the signature run of the Red Lodge resort. At the bottom of the run is a fairly steep part that they call the "face of M". It can be a little intimidating. Well we had gone up to the top and all the way down to the face without incident. At the face, Kari balked at the challenge and was telling her Dad she maybe couldn't do it. There is an easier way down but Paul was encouraging her to try. So she did. She put her skis parallel, faced them directly down the hill and took off. Paul saw her leave and headed out after her. Kari was just blazing down the face with Paul in hot pursuit. Kari went all the way down without turning. That in itself wouldn't be so bad. But the run makes a 90 degree turn to the right at the bottom of the face so directly in front of the face is a wall of trees and a couple other potential injury sites. Kari made it down and got stopped in the trees without hitting anything. A minor miracle in itself. Paul wasn't sure if he should be happy or mad. Just give her a hug Paul, come on!

One of the last few times I skied, human error, as well as my disease process I'm sure, almost cost me my life. I'm not being overly dramatic, this was close. It happened on, of all runs, probably my favorite run of all, Paradise, at Red Lodge. I was actually nearing the bottom of the run and noted a woman skiing in front of me quite slowly. She was breaking to her left pretty much right in front of me. The direction I was going favored my passing her on her left and it appeared she was about to turn back to her right. I hollered "On your left " and broke to her left. For some reason when I hollered, she broke off her turn to the right and turned back further left. I was moving faster than her and had already committed to the left, so I had to go even further left. I should have just stopped. But how bad could it be? She finally turned to her right but I was on the edge of the run and a ski caught the berm left by the groomer. It sucked me in and I remember throwing up my right hand up to deflect me from a tree. That apparently saved my life. I was knocked out cold as a carp. When I woke up, there was a young man standing near me asking me if I was okay. My right hand had deflected me enough that a tree only grazed my face but struck me in my chest, knocking me out and damaging my ribs. My face and right ear were bleeding, but that and my ribs were the extent of the injuries. I skied away from it, but that was as close to death that I knowingly have ever been. I think I only went skiing a couple more times after that and decided I had to hang it up.

Bob has never been one to hold his alcohol. On one trip to Red Lodge, when we stopped for lunch one day, for some reason it included these big bottles of German beer with our burgers. I've already talked about the grilling smell wafting up the hills and attracting all skiers. One thing that Red Lodge is well known for is their outdoor grilling at lunch. Anyway lunch that day included a couple of these big bottles of beer. I rode up with Bob on the triple after lunch and I couldn't believe my eyes. When we got to the top and dismounted, Bob took a tumble. That was new one to me, Bob falling while getting off the lift. Bob claimed it was the beer.

I think Red Lodge was always my wife, Gail's favorite. A couple green (beginner) runs, named Miami Beach and Ladies Aid were just made for her. Red Lodge is where my brother in law John tried a couple times to learn how to ski. After two or three days trying, he took a tumble in a creek, got wet and decided he'd had enough fun. He became a spectator.

CHAPTER 11

OUTDOORS

It is said that luck is when preparation and experience meets opportunity. So, if that's true and you are prepared and experienced and an opportunity arises, it really isn't luck that makes you successful. But people persist in using the word luck or lucky when referring to success in their hunting and fishing excursions when, in fact, there is no such thing. So, if you live in the outdoors as we do, you create your own luck, charisma, charm, kharma or whatever you want to call it. But then, there are those rare times when one of those words, inexplicably, puts you in the right place at the right time and….it's magic!

If you grew up in North Dakota in the fifties and sixties like I did, you were raised in a period when hunting just wasn't high on many priority lists. Those were simpler times; hunting and fishing had not yet evolved into the recreational industry it has become today. Hunting and fishing to put meat on the table had effectively ended forever with the end of WWII. It was a time when you could go hunting, even on a weekend, and not hear another shot. From the time our small group started hunting in the mid sixties until sometime in the eighties we pretty much had the area that we hunted to ourselves. There was no such thing as posted land and if someone did post for some odd reason, we were hometown kids and a quick stop to talk to them always got us where we needed to go. We were the uncrowned kings of our kingdom. Those were our golden years, when our love for the outdoors was born.

We grew up with guns, so our feelings about them are completely different than an inner city person. The city person looks at a gun as dangerous; something used for protection, to impose your will on someone else or to help steal someone else's valuables. Out here on the prairie we look at a gun as a tool to help us succeed in probably our single most popular pastime, hunting. Of course there are also quite a number of silhouette and target shooters also. Silhouette shooting is getting more popular all the time. Just as the name suggests, they shoot at metal silhouettes of animals, usually at very long ranges. It's quite a test of your shooting skills. While we have a healthy respect for a gun, we don't fear it. In fact it is just the opposite. We have to stay on guard so we don't become too cavalier with them. You tend to forget how dangerous guns can be. If you're a serious hunter, you most likely have several guns. If you're a gun affectionado like my brother Rob was, you may have a closet full.

There are almost endless outdoor opportunities available to us right out our backdoor! North Dakota has a couple premier walleye fisheries in Lake Sakakawea and Devils Lake. It also has the best waterfowl hunting in the lower 48. In what we call the "golden triangle", a triangular shaped area in the north central part of the state that starts at Minot, goes northwest to Kenmare and Bowbells, east to Bottineau and back southwest to Minot there are three large national wildlife refuges. They are, from west to east the Des Lacs, Upper Souris and Clark Salyer refuges. Together they host numbers of waterfowl that approach 1.5 to 2 million birds some falls. North Dakota has terrific whitetail deer hunting and better than average mule deer hunting. For upland game hunters there is fine sharptail grouse hunting, mostly in the western two thirds of the state, and tremendous pheasant hunting statewide. For residents only there is elk, moose and even bighorn sheep hunting on a once in a lifetime permit basis. I live in Bismarck, in the middle of all that. I can't imagine a better place to live for someone who's interested in the outdoors especially hunting and fishing, but it is also a great place for camping, bird watching, biking, hiking, swimming, jet skiing and almost anything else you can do outside.

After the mid-eighties, hunting started to change slowly but surely into an economic juggernaut. Hunting has also changed from a purely fun sport to a sport where too many people take it way too seriously. Because of the great fishing, waterfowl and upland hunting, North Dakota attracts non-resident hunters like ants to honey. The state tourism department uses hunting and fishing as one of the cornerstones of their advertising. That's good news for motel owners and restaurant operators, but it's really kind of sad news for us, but that's the way it is. The sad thing about this is that no matter what the resident hunters do, they are looked upon by some landowners and most small town business owners as a lower class of hunters as compared to the non-resident hunters. That's here in our own state. But, either you adapt to the changing times or quit. I'd like to think we did adapt to the changing landscape, and we've found and exploited the opportunities still available to us. I'm a little worried about the future of hunting, as money becomes more and more important. I fear it will result in fewer and fewer young people recruited to the sport and that will result in its eventual death. But enough doom and gloom, let's talk hunting and fishing.

Steele was a great place for an outdoorsman to grow up. We had excellent grouse hunting opportunities. For years, we had terrific Hungarian partridge hunting, something that has gone away with the "Big Wet" of the nineties and is just now recovering 13 years later. Duck hunting in the general area depends on precipitation amounts of course, but if you hunt the 'lakes' area southeast of Steele, there is at least some hunting all the time. About the time that I got out of high school (1970) geese suddenly started using the Steele area as a fall stopover and have continued to do so. Deer hunting over the years just gets better and better. In recent years there have been some tremendous bucks taken in the area.

If you're a hunter do you remember the first wild bird you bagged? If you do, I'm sure you remember how exciting it was! If you're not a hunter, I hope you can understand how excited an 11,12 or 13 year old can get now that's he's joined the hunting fraternity, especially one who's been around other hunters most of his life. I very clearly remember the first duck that I bagged. My Dad hunted a little and got me started hunting when I was around 11 years old. I'm a fall baby, so over the years I've celebrated my birthday by going duck hunting many times. One of those times was my 12th birthday. That day Dad came home from work and said he had been down to a local farmers place southeast of Steele for a tractor repair house call. He noticed some mallards were feeding in the farmer's cornfield. He didn't have to ask twice if I wanted to come along for an evening hunt. We had been in the field a short time when a flock of mallards came in. When Dad shouted, "take em", I sat up and I swung my .410 shotgun up. I was eyeball to eyeball with a greenhead. I shot and he folded. It seemed like the silly greenhead was sent to commit hari kari in front of me. I didn't even have to swing my gun or anything, all I did was cover him up and squeeze the trigger. So, it had started, and things would never be the same. I was a hunter, and it seemed like in no time at all, my brother Rob joined me in that fraternity.

In the field back in those days, Rob was my constant companion. He was a great companion; always ready to go wherever and to do whatever it took to get the job done. I have always loved the outdoors, but Rob's association with the outdoors was on a completely different level than mine. He was naturally very good at whatever the outdoors asked him to do. He was a crack shot, whether it was with a rifle or shotgun. He would pick up a fishing rod and immediately would catch the biggest fish. I think his outdoors prowess was due at least in part to his ability to focus completely on the task at hand. What I mean is that he was one of those guys that could run a half a mile and then hit the bullseye on a target shooting freehand at 250 yards. I know he could do it; because I've seen him do it, only with a live target. In fact I was with him when he shot a deer at 600-700 yards shooting freehand (without a gun rest), something that most shooters would consider nearly impossible! And he hit it with his first shot. It wasn't that hunting was the only thing in his life. He was married and had a family and they always came first. He could party with the best of them. He could and did work from sunrise to sunset. But put a gun in his hand and talk to him about going hunting somewhere and he would immerse himself in it completely. You didn't even have to ask him, you knew he was in on any hunting plans.

Which reminds me, do you know what a 'grock' is? Okay, how about a 'little brown thing with a pointy beak'? Well then, what is a 'silverware? I can see the confused look on your face, I'd better explain a little. Rob had a great imagination and he made up an alternate name for almost everything we encountered in the wild. A 'grock' was a bittern. A bittern is a water bird. When you flush a bittern, as it is rising up and flying away, it warbles out 'grooock'. A 'little brown thing with a pointy beak' was a snipe. That was an easy one. How about 'silverware'. If you think a little about waterfowl names eventually you run across the name Northern Shoveler, more commonly known as the spoonbill. Now you get it don't you? He had a hundred of them.

But Rob had a demon stalking him. Rob suffered from MS, the end result of which was his premature death at the age of 48 in late 2005. I not only lost a brother, I lost my best friend and the community of Steele lost a valuable part of itself. The Steele weekly paper had a column about Rob shortly after he died. The column was written by a local farmer's wife. Following are paraphrased excerpts from that column: "In Rob's case, he went from someone who was so active, to a man who could no longer enjoy the things he loved. He went from a man who probably walked miles in search of the perfect deer, to one who could no longer walk and relied on a wheelchair. He went from living in his home with the family he loved, to becoming a resident of a nursing home in his early 40's. It's not what Rob, his family or his friends wanted. As unfair as it seemed to many of us, that was what Rob had to face. It's hard to lose someone at only 48 years of age. Rob lived life as fully as he could have before the MS got him, and after it got him he lived his life with a quiet dignity and strength. I didn't know Rob well but that strength is what I'll always remember about him. Rob enriched the lives of many and will be missed dearly but never forgotten."

Waterfowl Hunting

When we talk about duck or goose hunting and say where we're going, or how we're going to hunt, my buddies and I understand each other completely. But I'm sure to most people it is a little confusing, so I'd better explain the terminology. In waterfowl hunting there are three hunting methods, you decoy, pass shoot or jump shoot. When you decoy, you usually scout in the late afternoon of the day before and find a stubble field where the ducks and/or geese are dining. They either eat waste grain like corn, peas, barley or green shoots from waste small grain (barley is their favorite) that has seeded itself and begins to grow if it is wet enough after the field is harvested. Then you go out to that field the next morning, set up decoys and attempt to attract the birds to the decoys when they return to feed. You also call to attract them as well as using the decoys. Decoying is my personal favorite hunting method. You can also decoy over water as well. In pass shooting you find a natural flyway for the birds, find a spot under that flyway and wait for the birds to start moving over you. Often times the birds are too high or if they're moving with the wind, flying to fast to effectively hunt them. Wind is really important with pass shooting. Jump shooting is when you find birds in a pond or field, try to sneak up close to them, and then try to shoot them as they jump off the ground or water. It is usually the most work if you have to sneak any distance.

We always considered ourselves better than average waterfowl hunters. In our young 'just turn us loose and we'll get some' days, Mom or Dad would take Rob and me out to one of the duck passes on Lake Etta (we mentioned how Lake Etta got its name a little earlier). We would get a ride out in the morning and we would sit there all day waiting for our chances. We always got a few. My Dad grew up on a farm on the shore of Lake Etta. Grandpa's farm was first settled and built up by Kidder County pioneer Ole Thompson just after the turn of the century. My Grandparents bought the farm from him in the mid to late 1920's and still lived there when we started hunting about 35 years later. Grandpa's place on Lake Etta was about 7 or 8 miles by road southeast of Steele. Lake Etta itself is a long skinny lake that begins a couple miles southeast of Dawson and angles southwest maybe 8-9 miles to where it ends, a couple miles east of straight south of Steele.

We would pass shoot at two spots where roads crossed the lake, in the middle by Grandpa's and at the southwest end near the three Koester farms. But our favorite pass was a point that stuck out from the north shore and extended almost halfway across the lake. It was about a half-mile southwest of Grandpa's. We would put waders on and would go out in the reeds at the end of the point. We used to get a little of everything. We bagged goldeneyes, buffleheads, ringnecks, redheads, canvasbacks, bluebills, mallards, pintails, blue wing teal, green wing teal, gadwalls, black ducks, shovelers and widgeons. In other words just about every species of duck you could find in North Dakota. Not all at once of course. We would only get a few birds a day, but we spent a lot of days out there. Our favorites were the crazy bluebills who always seemed like they couldn't get their act together. A dozen or so would come boiling over the point; we would shoot and knock a couple down. The bluebills would get 3 or 400 yards down the lake and they would turn around and come boiling back over us. Of course most ducks don't have a death wish and are a bit more wary.

The first success we had goose hunting, (and it was also the day I got my first goose) was in 1970. I came back from college on a weekend in October to do a little hunting. Okay, okay, there may have been a girl involved too, but that's another story. When I got home, Rob told me he had found a small flock of snow geese feeding in a stubble field toward the west end of Lake Etta. Rob had saved up about 30-40 white bleach bottles just waiting for this chance. He had painted black wing tips on the jugs and also had carved Styrofoam goose heads for them. The next morning we hauled them out to the field in the dark in the trunk of the car. There we set them out in the field as decoys. When it got light about 5 or 6 snow geese came into our "spread" and we got 2 of them. A short while later, a larger bunch came in and we got 4 more. That was it, but we were tickled to death. I walked back to get the car and I'll never forget that when I started the car, the Beach Boys were singing "Be True To Your School" on the radio. It's funny how some things stick in your mind.

Those bleach bottles disappeared long ago. They were the very first goose decoys we had and have since been replaced with hundreds of decoys, enough to fill a 6 foot by 14 foot enclosed trailer. Those were certainly simpler days.

What we called the Alkali Flats is a large salty water area across a ridge to the southeast of Lake Etta. When the geese moved into the area, Rob and I discovered that there was a natural flow of birds from the Alkali Flats to the northeast, to

Black Slough and the Slade National Wildlife Refuge and back the other way to the Alkali Flats. Black Slough is a large slough that is situated between Slade refuge and the Alkali Flats. In pre-historic years the water on the Alkali Flats had been much higher. There were lake banks far above the current water level. We called that lake bank area on the northeast end of the flats, 'the pass'. Within our own little circle if you said "the pass" everyone knew where you meant.

One morning a few years after the bleach bottle hunt, Rob and I were on the pass. We had bagged a few ducks but no geese yet. A bunch of geese was sort of flying toward us but for some reason they veered way off to our west. Rob stood up and jacked the shell out of the chamber of his Browning. He fished a 00-buckshot shell out of his pocket and loaded it into his gun. He swung way out ahead of the geese and fired. He stood there for two or three seconds, it seemed, and as we watched, a goose folded up and fell to the ground. We paced off the distance from where Rob was standing to the bird. It was 187 steps! If you know anything about shooting a shotgun, you know that hitting and killing a bird (even though this was the lead shot era) beyond 80 or 90 steps (yards) is almost impossible! I'll also tell you there are only nine large lead pellets in a 00-buck or as Rob used to call them a "double naught spy shell", another of his special names. Where did that name come from? To Jethro Bodine of the Beverly Hillbillies television series a zero was called a naught. He called James Bond a "double naught spy" because of his 007 code name. So Rob just adapted Jethro's name for Bond to the 00-buckshot shells. Kind of complicated, but very simple!

While hunting on the pass around the same time as Rob's "shot" on kind of a cold, slow morning, I had an unusual encounter. I was laying in kind of a washout in the old lakebank waiting for a goose. I heard footsteps behind me, turned my head and there was a little whitetail buck about two feet away, trying to smell me. When I said "Hi" he got a startled look on his face, froze for a second or two and then turned and ran. I think he was spooked. He hasn't called, written or come over since!

I've got a couple other stories from the pass, but they both involve violations of game and fish laws so I'd better not tell them. Okay, okay, but only one of them. The statute of limitations has more than likely expired. Rob and I were having a pretty good day on the pass. We just about had a limit of mallards; we had some snow geese and also three Canadians, which was one over our limit. I don't remember why we had an extra Canadian, if it was a mistake or what the circumstances were. There had been a pickup driving slowly back and forth and stopping for a few minutes at a time on a road visible to us. We didn't recognize the pickup and we were pretty sure that we were being watched by a game warden with a spotting scope. When we left the pass to go back to our vehicle we formulated an emergency plan. It went like this. As we walked back to our pickup we walked through a short dip where we were out of sight of the pickup watching us for about 20-30 seconds. When we hit the dip I dropped a Canadian goose out of my right hand and into a badger hole which Rob immediately replaced with a mallard from the game pouch in my jacket. We didn't miss a step and just kept on walking. As we approached our vehicle a federal game warden stepped out from behind a haystack, identified himself and asked to see our birds. He went through them twice, he was sure he had us, but he didn't. He was a nice guy and we talked to him for quite a while before he took off. Sorry warden. Incidentally, we went back out and picked up the goose, it didn't go to waste.

If we talked about the Redhead pass, that was a completely different spot. I guess if you weren't one of us you needed a scorecard to keep track of things. By the same token if you talked about "the point" our group knew that it was the spot mentioned earlier southwest of our Grandpas. We hunted a lot over a large area and did a lot of pass shooting. The pass, the Redhead pass, the point, the north point, the north road, the south road, the south pass, the fence line, the hayfield, north and south Weber and the north pass. Mentioning any of those to our small group brought an instant knowing smile. We had great memories of all of them. Some were duck passes, some goose passes, some were both.

The Redhead pass was miles away from the pass, somewhere in the neighborhood of 15 miles. It was on the land of friend and schoolmate, Jeff. The Redhead pass was on a ridge that separated a large slough from huge Horsehead Lake (from the air the lake looked much like a horse's head, with the nose pointed east, toward Jeff's place). Sometimes it was an amazing place, where I'm sure a few hunters could have easily taken 40 to 50 redheads back in the old days. The limit when we hunted there was usually 2 per hunter and of course we never exceeded the limit. Honest! Up at Jeff's place there was another pass that we occasionally frequented, the north pass. We had days when 6 or 8 guys would take limits that included nearly every species of duck imaginable on that pass.

From about 1980 until around 1985, Rob and his family lived on a farm on the south side of the Slade National Wildlife Refuge. Because of that, during those years we did a lot of hunting in the area south of Slade. One day at the end of October we were sitting along the refuge fence trying to pass shoot some snow geese (remember our discussion about the names of our pass shooting spots. Remember "the fenceline"). The geese weren't cooperating with us. They just weren't flying. Sometimes as it gets later in the season the geese fly later and later in the morning and sometimes not at all until afternoon. These geese were in the latter category. This particular day the Game and Fish allowed an extra hour of hunting moving the closing time from 1 to 2 PM. This also happened to be the day that daylight savings time ended, in effect adding another hour for a total of two more hours of goose hunting. I don't know if one of the geese had a watch or if they were using a sundial, but 5 minutes after what would have been 1 PM, the quitting time of the day before, the geese just started pouring off the refuge. We had fabulous shooting for those extra two hours. The geese either had forgotten to get a copy of the waterfowl regulations or had lost them.

There were a couple of severe drought years in the late 80's. In fact, they were so severe that not much grain was harvested in the Steele area. If you planted wheat or barley those two years, it was so dry that if the seeds germinated the plants would get about six inches tall, head out and form whatever grain it could and die. It certainly wasn't harvestable. But there was enough grain in those fields to attract geese and ducks to them in the fall. I remember one windy dusty day; my brother Darin was goose hunting with some of his buddies a few miles east of Steele. I don't remember what I was doing that day, but late in the morning, I was driving past the field they were in. I decided to drive out and see how they were doing. When I got out in the field, Darin came over to talk to me. He looked like one of those old white actors made up to look like a black man; his face was so dirty. He would have been invisible at night if his eyes were closed. I just had to laugh when he walked up.

Early in the waterfowl season of 1998, I was hunting by myself one morning. I had decided the afternoon before to hunt what we called Vic's Slough. Yes, it's the same Vic. This particular slough also was a good deer hunting spot. Vic let us post it to save it for ourselves, much to the chagrin of another local, let's call him 'Gene', but that's another story in itself. Anyway, I got out there that morning and it was overcast and very dark. I drove down to the slough and dropped off decoys and equipment that I would need. I drove the pickup some distance away and parked it, careful to note a distant light that I would use as a guide to get back to the slough.

I got out of the pickup and headed for the light and after about three or four minutes slammed into a big round bale that knocked the wind out of me and knocked me down. Needless to say I walked the rest of the way with my arms extended out in front of me and of course then encountered no more roadblocks. For the want of a flashlight the hunt was almost spoiled. Now I always carry a flashlight. Oh yeah, the hunting was wonderful.

'Gene' always considered himself a better hunter than we were. Whether or not he was is not an issue. He always had to have the best spots for his hunting grounds. He was always worried that we would do better than him so he was always watching us. When we were allowed to post Vic's slough, it must have ticked him off, because he wrote nasty notes to us on the signs. He was a perfect example of one of those guys that took hunting way too seriously. Most of us grew up but he never did.

The same year, in the same slough, one day I took buddy Paul and his son, Chris, along duck hunting. We had put some decoys out and had settled in for an afternoon hunt. Chris was about 10 years old and it was his first time hunting so he was excited. I listened to his dad give him a sermon about the decoys. He told him that they weren't his and that he should be careful not to shoot any of them. We hadn't been there very long when a duck, I think it was a teal, came and landed on the edge of the decoys. Now the boy was really excited and was whispering to his dad that he wanted to take a shot at it. After a little begging, his dad relented and he took careful aim and shot. Apparently the aim wasn't all that good because when he shot, about four decoys flew up in the air and the duck, unharmed, flew away. In order to put Chris and his Dad at ease, I hollered over immediately something like "That's okay Chris, you'll get him next time". The decoys were just things, and the young man's pride was a lot more important than they were.

A couple years ago I demonstrated the prowess of the "widow maker" (motorized flapping wing duck decoy). As it turned out the demo was only for myself. It is quite a hunting tool. I had scouted one evening in late October and found a field with maybe a couple thousand mallards feeding in it. The next morning with 2 or 3 other guys, we decoyed in that field. A week earlier we had hunted mallards that were feeding in a field in the same area. The mallards didn't come back (at least not early) the next morning and that day we left the field empty handed. I had a sneaking suspicion that they wouldn't show up early the next morning this time either. I did feel, however that they would show up sometime, probably later in the morning. As it gets later in the season, mallards (and geese too) get a little unpredictable. Well, my feeling was right; the ducks didn't show up early the next morning. The other guys left, but I had decided to wait the mallards out for a while. Wild ducks are like tomorrow, both come without warning. About 10 or 10:30 I was sitting there admiring the weather (it was a sunny, bright, blue sky day) when I heard the roar that wings of ducks make when rapidly losing altitude. I hit the remote button and turned the widow maker on, as soon as I heard the wings. There were about 75-100 mallards dropping out of the sky and screaming into the decoys. They came right down on the deck. That same scene was repeated a few more times over the next hour or so. I took one greenhead from each bunch and in the end I had a limit. I love it when a plan comes together!

There's one neat thing about field shooting in central North Dakota; the fields come equipped with blinds. Blinds? Well, technically they're called rockpiles and they serve a dual purpose, hiding hunters and clearing the land of rocks so it can be farmed. Now you've got to wonder, in the grand scheme of things, were the rocks put there to help hunters or torment farmers? It's one question learned people have been debating for decades. It's similar to what came first the chicken or the egg. I'd like to apologize to the learned people for dragging them down to my level. If they ever actually sat and debated what the real purpose of the rocks was, they'd have to have way too much time on their hands.

The "Big Wet" started in central North Dakota in 1993. Way above average rainfall that summer ushered in several wetter than normal years, more or less culminating with the record snowfall in the winter of 96-97. Because of that local duck production shot way up. It wasn't until 2005 that the last of the inundated wetlands dried up. In late September of 1994 we had almost finished harvest but still had about 70-80 acres of wheat standing on a quarter of Dad's land southeast of Steele. That it was still standing was the only thing that saved it when something like seven inches of rain fell on it one day. We were able to get all but about an acre or two that was in a low-lying flooded area. On opening weekend of waterfowl season a week or so later, that patch of wheat with standing water in it was full of ducks. We got a bunch of mallards and pintails both days that opening weekend. You couldn't have beaten them out of that wheat patch with hand grenades. That was the first of several years of exceptional duck hunting. Incidentally, later that fall in the same flooded wheat patch, I shot at three greenheads coming into the wheat patch. I got all three with one shot, the only time I've done that.

That was until this year. We were on a pass, up at buddy Jeff's place that I'd never been on before. You've seen Jeff's name before, earlier in this chapter. We were having what was one of our all-time great hunts that we have had on any pass. That's saying a lot, because of the amount of hunting we've done over the years. Five widgeons (species of duck) approached me from the south. I hunkered down and when they got over me, I drew on the leader of the five and touched one off. I couldn't believe it when the first four dropped. I picked up three of the four, one escaped. Better to be lucky rather than good. This particular hunt, we didn't have just one or two ducks passing over us at a time, sometimes it was a hundred or more.

I will have to admit that in spite of the glut of non resident hunters, in the last few years, I've had a couple other outings, in addition to the one above, that resulted in some of the best waterfowl hunting I've ever had in the Steele area. One of those outings was when I decoyed in barley stubble southeast of Steele about 5 or 6 years ago. I hunted in the same field for three days straight. It was incredibly easy. I was very choosy and still limited out each day with mallard greenheads, drake pintails and large Canadian geese in an hour or less. A third fabulous hunt was when I pass shot mallards in wind and snow northwest of Steele. The ducks were leaving a slough and flying up a valley in a stubble field to try to stay out of the wind. I took a limit of greenheads mallards in about 90 seconds. I honestly could have shot a hundred or more. The opportunities are there; you just got to spend the time in the field to find them and then go after them.

Over the years we have found that the two most favorable weather conditions for successful waterfowl hunting are wind and snow, in that order. If it's snowy and windy and there are available birds, you've just about got a sure thing. In hunting circles there's an old adage, "If you hunt in the rain you just get wet", so I usually find something else to do on rainy days.

Goose camp

It was in about 1987 that we started a tradition that has lasted quite some time, in fact we still do it in a slightly altered form. We chose a week in late October when we could all get together and we invited guests in for a week of waterfowl hunting. We've always called it "goose camp". Initially it was based at Mark's parent's house in Steele. It has continued over the years moving back and forth between Steele, Kenmare, Minot, and Mohall. Then in 2003, with the snow geese hanging in Saskatchewan a lot longer than they used to, it moved north of the border to Saskatchewan.

That first year, the goose hunting was a little bleak at the beginning of the hunt, but we did have some very good duck hunting, thanks to Jeff and his duck passes. The last morning of the hunt, we split into two groups with Marks group decoying for snow geese and my group going after Canadas. I think Mark's group got about a dozen snows and blues while my bunch got about 8 or 9 Canadian geese, so we ended our first goose camp on a high note.

In October of 1988, one of our most memorable days ever unfolded south of Dawson (7 miles east of Steele). It was the second year of our 'goose camp'. The area we were hunting that morning was closed to the hunting of Canadian geese. The area was home to a nesting flock of giant Canadians that was being established near and on the Slade National Wildlife Refuge. It was closed to protect those resident geese. We were trying to get whitefront and snow geese. So, the Canadians were semi-tame and we had dozens of them land in the decoys. One of our guests, Joe, put a decoy on his own head and was trying to crawl up to and grab one of the geese that had landed in the decoys. The goose would honk a little and waddle away from him and couldn't figure out what was going on. At times we would have literally thousands of Canadian geese circling just above us. When we would spot and shoot at groups of whitefronts or snow geese, what do you suppose the Canadian geese did? Well, you're right if you guessed the first thing they did was crap. It was raining goose crap much of the morning. One of our hunters picked out and knocked down a black brant out of all the geese that went over him. He said it just looked different so he went for it. A black brant is a west coast sea goose (he was way off course). What he was doing there we had no idea. The guy that shot it didn't want it, so I kept it and took it to the taxidermist. He wasn't the only one in the area though, my youngest brother who hunted with his own group in those days, also got a brant that fall in the area south or southeast of Steele. The next fall Rob and I were decoying west of Steele and we had a small group of black brant approach the decoys. We didn't get any but they were definitely there the next fall too. The memory of that morning that stands out most clearly in my mind is one of Rob. About mid-morning he had to take a whiz. He stood up to do so and as he was answering natures call about six snow and blue geese that had snuck into the decoys passed directly over him about 10 feet above his head. You should have seen him scramble! That morning was the best whitefront hunting we've ever had.

During one of our first "goose camps", Rob brought a swan over to the house that he had harvested during the first modern day swan hunt that same year. He had picked and prepared it for roasting. He asked Mark's mother, Elaine, if she would prepare it for one of our dinners, which she graciously did. We were all gathered at the table when she brought it in. It looked scrumptious. We sliced off some breast meat and passed it around. It was inedible! Since that day I've tried to prepare swan every way that I know and it's just terrible. Not even the magic of bacon can save it. That is one meat to avoid at a wild game feed if at all possible. I've actually read stories about how good to eat they are. They can't be writing about the same bird.

In 2001 we were hunting during goose camp week out of Mohall north of Minot. The goose hunting left a lot to be desired, so we expanded our scouting area to include areas off the Clark Salyer refuge (further southeast), where we had been told there were more mallards. We found a barley field southeast of Newburg that was just loaded with feeding mallards. The next morning, three other goose campers and I went into that field and once more witnessed the power of the 'widow maker'. We were sitting in that field with a few decoys out, including the before mentioned 'widow maker'.

A bunch of mallards would approach the field way up in the air, I would turn on the 'widow maker' and they would just dump all the air off their wings and bomb in. When ducks or geese dump air they actually turn over and keep flipping back and forth. It is one of the neatest things you'll ever see. They literally drop out of the sky. We got a bunch of mallards that morning. The 'widow maker' (motorized duck decoy) legend among the goose campers was born that day. We already knew what it could do!

About a year or so either way from that mallard shoot, we were in Mohall for goose camp. A snowstorm had hit and driven about three-quarters of the birds south, how far we didn't know. So we decided to pack up and head south to the Steele area and hunt there for two or three days. I headed south with a load of decoys by myself and missed a turn that I wanted to make, so I headed south at Drake, ND intending to backtrack a little cross country to my road. Well, I was working my way southwest and was on a good gravel road that changed to a "low maintenance" road. Then it changed to a section line trail, then to just tracks in grass. Finally I was out in a CRP (Conservation Reserve Program) field that was so rough I couldn't hang onto the steering wheel. About a third of a mile ahead of me there was a grove of trees, so I headed for them. When I got close enough, I could see a split in the trees and I headed for that. I went through the split and found myself in a farmyard. I kept going past a house with a picture window facing toward me and there was an old farmer standing in front of the window watching me. I just kept going down his driveway to the main road and never looked back. I still remember the amazed look on that old fellow's face. I'm sure he was wondering, "just where did that idiot come from"?

One of the last years we hunted north of Minot, I was hauling a load of decoys north in the wee hours of the morning. The intention was to get north of Minot before daybreak to scout for our first hunt of camp, which would take place the next morning. The rest of the guys would be arriving during the day. I was cruising along with a heavily loaded pickup and was approaching Washburn about 40 miles north of Bismarck. I was about to go over the second of two bridges just south of Washburn when I noticed that the highway was covered with deer at the other end of the bridge. I hit the brakes, feeling that it wasn't going to be a question of whether I was going to hit a deer, but of how many I was going to hit. As I was sliding to a stop I could see deer flashing by on both sides. When I got stopped a small whitetail buck was standing only inches away from the pickup hood looking in the front windshield. Somehow I had missed every deer. I had to get out and walk around the pickup a couple times until the adrenaline rush passed.

That same hunt, we were staying in a motel at Mohall, almost straight north of Minot. Outside of our room sitting under an overhang and on the cement sidewalk was a chest type freezer. I opened it up when I got to the motel and saw it had a few geese and ducks in it. For the next two or three days I put cleaned birds in it to freeze and store until we went home. About the fourth day we were there, we got back to the motel after scouting in the early evening. We pulled up to our room and the freezer was gone. I went to the office and asked where they had moved their freezer. With a surprised look on his face, the clerk said they didn't have one, but, he said, if you're talking about the one that was outside your room, that one belonged to the guys next to you and they hauled it back to Minnesota just after noon today. I bet they were surprised when the got home and divvied up the birds. I hope I didn't get them in trouble!

In 2002 my wife Gail and I made our first trip to Saskatchewan to waterfowl hunt. Originally I was going to go with a group from Kansas, but at the very last minute they cancelled. I already had my license and so I told my wife I was going anyway even if I had to go alone. She told me that if I would wait to take off until Thursday, she would take a couple days off from school and she would go with me. So I did and we did. We hunted Friday and Saturday. When we arrived in the Foam Lake, SK (about 450 miles almost straight north of Bismarck) area we fairly quickly found geese. When we asked for permission to hunt on Friday morning, we received it with a condition. We thought, oh no, what do we have to do, help castrate pigs? The condition turned out to be that if we hunted in the morning on their land, we would have to haze the geese out of a swathed oats field that afternoon to which we readily agreed. So we ended up hunting both the morning and a little bit in the afternoon on Friday. I think we got about a dozen geese or so that day.

The lady we talked with to get permission to hunt was pretty funny. The stubble that the geese were in was fenced and there were cattle in the field. When we were given permission I reminded her that there were cattle in the field, with the intention of reassuring her we would be careful. Before I finished making my point, she cut in and reassured me that we didn't need to be afraid of the cattle, she didn't think that they would hurt us.

On Saturday, hunting in a different area, I got about 10 geese in the morning and then didn't want to take any more, but I kept the decoys in the field. The way the geese poured into those decoys was amazing. That was the only time that I had snow geese landing in decoys. I think Gail and I probably had the best time together on that hunt that I've or should I say we've ever had on a hunting trip.

The last few years we have taken the goose camp north of the border. Hunting in Canada has been a hoot. You would never think in your wildest dreams that Saskatchewan would be so different. There's not a wall separating our countries. In North Dakota just about everybody that owns a pickup has a four-wheel drive. You would think north of the border it would be more so, but no, most people drive two-wheel drive pickups, that they call their "half ton". Virtually all gas stations are full service; you don't pump your own gas. Of course they sell gas by the liter instead of by gallons. Not everyone talks like a guide we met last fall, every other word he uttered was bloody or eh (pronounced like a long A). I'm not sure if that's the proper Canadian spelling of the word. But the word "eh" becomes very prominent as soon as you cross the border. Every small town you drive through has an indoor or outdoor hockey arena, hockey is king. Another big difference is that they seem to like tasteless food and they like to put gravy on everything. You never know what to order in a restaurant. But to their credit they are without a doubt the hardest working people I've ever known. And for the most part they are the friendliest people you'll ever meet, not all of them, you'll definitely run into a few American haters. They've usually got a good reason. Most of the Canadian landowners, if they tell you no for whatever reason, feel bad about it and always explain why their answer was what it was. This year we had a landowner find us out in the field while we were hunting. She found us to tell us to call before we come up next year and we could have exclusive hunting rights on her land. Talk about a gracious host!

Probably our best day of snow goose hunting in Saskatchewan occurred this past fall (2006) near the town of Wadena, north of the Quill Lakes, when we hunted our first morning in a barley field and took about 50 birds.

Big Game Hunting

Rob lived for about five years just outside the Slade National Wildlife Refuge south of Dawson. Because it was so near his house we did some deer hunting on the Slade Refuge. One day on the refuge we were hunting along a ridge and we spotted a hunter in front of us with a downed deer lying in front of him. When we got closer, we noticed the hunter was throwing his knife at the deer, over and over. Every time he threw the knife, he jumped back. When we got to the hunter we discovered that he was a young man who told us he was on his first hunt. It turned out his Dad had told him if he got a buck he was supposed to cut the throat, a rather grisly affair and an operation the young man didn't know how to perform. So being the good guys we are, although we don't do it, we showed him how to cut the throat, helped him field dress it, tied a piece of rope onto the antlers and sent the young man on his way. To this day it just amazes me, when I think about that young fellow, that his father had just let him go off by himself like he did. I found that with my son, being with him when he bagged game was, for me, a large and satisfying part of the experience. I always wanted to share the excitement and to hear about the shot he made or what happened up to the kill. There are always things that you want to share with someone.

So, it should be clear to everyone by now, hunting was Rob's passion. He continued to hunt as long and as hard as he could. One of the last hunts he went on where he was still capable of participating fully was an elk hunt with our brother-in-law out in Montana. That was in the late 80's. He hunted with us for several years after that, but every year became a little harder. Back to the Montana elk hunt...Rob had done a little pre-hunt 'strategizing' and had come up with an idea for a urinal that would save on getting up and going outside in the middle of the night. So he brought a small funnel and a piece of garden hose along. The first night we were in camp, I heard him get out of his bag, grab his "urinal" and it worked like it was advertised. The second night he grabbed his urinal again and began to use it. In a few seconds I heard him swearing and also heard the sound of water splattering on the tarp we used for a floor. He had forgotten one of the basic laws of physics. If you cool a liquid below its freezing point, it changes states, changing from a liquid to a solid, in this case creating a pretty good plug. So the moral of the story is one that you'll immediately recognize: "Always drain your hose in cold weather, especially if you're using it for personal hygiene."

The same trip, a night or two later, I was again awakened way too early by one of my roomies. My brother-in-law John was also sleeping in the tent with Rob and me. Now, why, on a cold night would someone, while sleeping, crawl completely out of his sleeping bag? That's what I was wondering when I heard John complaining he was cold and when I turned on my flashlight and looked over at him, saw that he was completely out of his sleeping bag and he had it draped sideways across his body. That must have been one heck of a dream! He had no idea how he had gotten into his predicament.

Speaking of dreams, one of the other guys along with us on the hunt told me about a dream he had one night in camp. He dreamt that he woke up one morning and lifted the flap on his tent. There standing in plain sight were two big bull elk. He quickly grabbed his gun and somehow managed to get both of them. When he walked over to them, they were both about the size of a large dog. The mind does strange things once in a while. Another hunting partner also had a strange one. It seems he had a D8 Caterpillar bulldozer that he used to help irrigate. He raised sugar beets in the Yellowstone valley. He had a neighbor who coveted that dozer and had been trying to buy it for some time. The dream was that he was talking to his neighbor and the neighbor offered him $500 for the bulldozer and Bud (our hunting partner) told him no, that was way too much! It must have been the altitude or the food (or the beer?). Bud passed away a few years ago. He was a great guy.

I hunt a lot now with a friend, Mark, who I swear, carries a deer magnet somewhere in a pocket or pouch. I've hunted whitetails a lot and taken a lot of bucks, but I bet on average the

B & C score of his average buck is probably double my average. The Boone and Crockett (B&C) score is a standardized way to compare the size of one animal's antlers to another. He's got a number of terrific whitetail bucks mounted and continues to find more of them. During our last two Black Hills hunts he has taken two way above average bucks for the Hills. I don't know what he does different, but I would like to find out, bottle it and sell it.

Marks Dad, Tom, was always giving us crap about spending so much time hunting. He would say, "Hunting, humpf, nobody ever made a living hunting!". I don't quite know how to write that disgusted sound he used to make. Tom was a great guy, he never fooled us with his gruffness. For some reason he always had to try and jerk us around. We always thought it was his round about way of showing affection. Tom died way too young. He died of ALS (Lou Gehrig's disease) just two or three years after he retired.

When we were young we deer hunted religiously in a small area southeast of Steele. During those years we had a few traditions that to many will sound juvenile and a little silly. That's because they were juvenile and a little silly. But we were just kids and were starting our own traditions. We weren't aware of a 'tradition handbook' if there was one. One of our traditions was every season we started our hunt at Vic's slough. Another was we toasted every kill by passing around a jug of fruit flavored Sloe Gin and everyone took a sip. Another was every deer we killed was loaded into a pickup and taken to the "guttin tower", a specific electrical highline tower, to be field dressed. We also always hunted our butts off with the intention of filling all out tags by noon on Sunday of opening weekend. If we found a deer with big horns that was great, but in those days it was quite an accomplishment to just get a buck. But you know, over the years, we've found that tradition is a very large part of hunting. That's what makes it so special to so many of us.

Let's mix a little beauty in with the beast. My hunting buddy, Bob, has a sister, Marlyce, who at least in her younger days (I haven't seen her since we were in college together) was a drop dead gorgeous, tall blonde. She was pretty enough to participate in beauty contests and also has a daughter that won the Miss Wyoming title! I knew her quite well because she and Bob went to school in Steele during our grade school days. Their family moved and she and Bob finished school in Bismarck. Many years later, when Marlyce and I were both in college at NDSU in Fargo, I ran into her one day. This is the story of that meeting. I was in the lounge in the Student Union with a half dozen buddies. We were showing our maturity level and were being quite noisy. While we were carrying on, I happened to notice Marlyce approaching us through the hallway that runs north and south past the lounge. I was watching her approach (a great joy in itself I might add) and my greatest hope was that she would see me. She did, and as she was walking by, she smiled and said "Hi Ken", and kept on walking. You could have heard a pin drop. She made my day.

By the way, Bob and Marlyce's mothers name is Lennis, the only other person named Lennis in the world that I've heard of other than my sister. You've got to admit it's not a common name.

We used to go deer hunting in the Black Hills every fall. It's hard to explain why, but the Black Hills quickly became very familiar to us and going to the hills every fall was like going home, even though we had to drive 350 miles from home to get there. As far as out of state deer hunts went, it was so nice because up until around 1990 you could still buy nonresident licenses to deer hunt in the Black Hills over the counter. Because of that, you could make plans well in advance knowing you would get tags.

In 1986 we decided we would like to try and camp during our deer hunt down there. So in November of 1986 we took off with Mark's cousin Bob Thompson's camper. We had a great time and all too quickly filled all our tags. After we finished we had a celebration that ended up with us out by the meat pole under the stars toasting Buck (a coyote), Little Buck, Young Buck, Big Buck, and Old Buck (we normally don't name the deer we get, you'll have to excuse us, we were very inebriated, or as Rob so eloquently put it, we were 'woozy from the boozy').

Mark shot the coyote we got on that 1986 Black Hills hunting trip. Mark was on a ridge near camp and was 'pussy footing' (sneaking), as Marks Uncle Rusty calls it, down the ridge. I was paralleling the ridge and had spotted the coyote almost as soon as we started our little drive. I was watching it and saw it was about to cross a little clearing. I found a rest for my gun and sighted in on the clearing. The coyote popped into my scopes field of view and I was squeezing the trigger, when BOOM, a shot rang out that killed the coyote and scared the crap out of me. What are the chances that both Mark and I the spotted the coyote and decided to shoot it at almost exactly the same instant? Apparently quite good.

We took the camper back down to the Black Hills a couple falls later. On the way to our camping spot Mark and I were in his pickup pulling the camper as we went through the hills. We weren't very far along on our journey through the hills, just a couple miles south of the highway. We were singing along with a country music station. In other words, we weren't paying real close attention to the road. We missed a sharp turn and cut straight across a U in the road and ended up right back on the road on the other side of the U with no harm done. Rob and Bob were behind us in Rob's pickup. When we left the road Bob nearly had a heart attack (remember the camper was his). When we got the pickup stopped, Bob was on us like a fly on feces. It wouldn't have been so bad but we had already had a propane tank come out of its holder, fall off of the camper and bounce down the highway while going through the Spearfish Canyon. We just had to stand there and weather the storm.

Maybe 25 years ago, probably one of the first times we deer hunted in the Black Hills, we were in a group lead by Mark's Uncle, Rusty. Rusty is a no nonsense, my way or the highway kind of guy, mainly because he didn't want any of us to get hurt or lost in the Hills. Rusty is a Finlander who grew up deer hunting, practically for a living, on the Upper Peninsula of Michigan. He taught us how to hunt one ridge at a time. We called each of the particular ridge hunts a drive. Most of the ridges had been given names by the group over the years. Frying Pan, John Deere, Aspen, the Knob, the 117 Knob, East and West ridges are a few of the names. Basically the way it worked is if you had five guys for instance, you would spread three or four of them out across the ridge and they would hunt the ridge down hill or from highest to lowest. One or two guys would be at the bottom of the ridge to block avenues of deer escapes. When everyone got to the bottom, the drive was over and everyone was trucked back to the top where again three or four hunters were deployed to drive the next ridge and the other one or two would drive the vehicle to the bottom to block. Obviously not all ridges have good enough access to be hunted this way. Rusty also taught us which ones we could hunt easiest, along with the best spots to block escape routes.

This is the story of one of those drives that went a little awry. We had started a drive, one that wasn't very familiar to some of us. It just happened that Mark, Rob and I were side by side at the left end of the drivers. At some point we separated from the line and drifted further to the left. We hadn't even noticed we were separated. Then we jumped a buck. It took us a little further to our left. We usually hunt on the west side of the Hills right on the South Dakota/Wyoming border (you'll understand why I told you this very soon). We got the buck and when no one else from the group responded to our shooting we realized we were just slightly lost. We weren't really lost, we just didn't know exactly where we were. We field dressed the deer and decided by committee where we had to go to get back to a road. We pulled and pulled and pulled some more. Finally, up ahead, there was Rusty and his vehicle. We didn't know if we should be happy or scared. When we got the deer closer he hollered at us in his Finlander brogue "I tink you guys in Wyoming". Oh great, we had not only gotten lost but we may have poached a deer. We got the deer to his vehicle and he read us the riot act up one side and down the other. I remember fellow Steelite and long time hunting buddy Kenny Mack standing behind Rusty making faces at us while Rusty was chewing us out. We would have liked to have strangled him that day. I don't know about the other two guys, but I was much more careful after that.

Let's head back to South Dakota, where we were on another one of our Black Hills deer hunts. It was nearing dark and Mack and I were road hunting on a trail that they call the Sherwood Springs road. As we were driving along we noticed that up ahead of us were two hunters walking on the edge of the road. The road winds around but heads generally south. We had already driven all the way in to the end of the Springs road and were on our way back out. We had not noticed any vehicles on the way in or out. We slowly passed the hunters and Mack noticed one of them gave us kind of a desperate look, although neither said anything. We were past them and we looked at each other and said almost simultaneously, "We better stop". So we stopped and asked if they needed a lift. They happily accepted our offer but they told us they had no idea where they wanted to go, they were lost. Their story was they were from Colorado and were hunting with a buddy from Rapid City. They had arrived and set up camp in the dark. That morning after a few brief instructions from their South Dakota buddy, the three of them headed out in three different directions,,,in the dark.

One of them shot a coyote during the day and sometime that afternoon, somehow the two Colorado hunters had run into each other. Neither had a clue where they were. When we found them they were headed in a southerly direction as we noted earlier. We asked them to describe where they shot the coyote, describe where their camp was and what kind of vehicle they had come in on. To their amazement we knew where both the coyote and their camp were. We went and picked up their coyote and then in the dark took them to their camp. We have spent so much time hunting in that area, we know practically every nook and cranny in the Sherwood-Kinney-Thompson Canyon area. Their camp was in the Kinney Canyon. When we had initially found the two hunters, the southerly direction that they were going was taking them farther and farther from their camp. A worried hunting buddy was waiting for them. He gladly fed us most of their beer. We gladly drank it. Don't you just love a happy ending!

The last couple trips we've made to the Black Hills, four of us have stayed at a Forest Service cabin that they rent out up by a fire lookout tower, just a few miles west of Forest Service Road 117, almost right on the South Dakota-Wyoming border. It's been a real enjoyable experience, one that I hope to repeat as long as I still can. The only down side to that is that we have to do our own cooking, but as long as they don't allow me close to the stove, we should be fine.

In 1996 Mark and I were treated to an elk hunt in the Greybull River basin in northwestern Wyoming. That elk hunt with Mark, Gordy, myself, cook Ron and his Rothweiler, Jake, was the kind of hunt that everyone should get a chance to experience.

We took horses in 19 miles from a trailhead on the Greybull River south of Cody, Wyoming to a campsite called Half Cabin located on a drainage called Venus Creek. Why do they call it Half Cabin? I'd like to tell you some strange and exotic story about pioneers, trappers and Indians. There isn't one, it's just the site of an unfinished cabin.

I have to do a little backtracking and explaining before I go on. Gordy is one of our goose camp buddies. Out of the goodness of his heart, he told Mark and me that if we got drawn for bull elk tags in the Greybull area he would take care of setting up a camp for us and serve as our guide. We would just have to pay for food and our tags. Well, we were drawn, and Gordy and a buddy of his set up the camp for us and got Ron to cook for us.

When we were on our way in, about 2/3 of the way to the camp, we stopped and spiked (slept out under the stars). We spiked so we could hunt an area the next morning where Gordy had spotted a big bull elk when they put the camp in. We lit a fire and Gordy threw a big 'pitch' stump (Gordy called it a 'pitch' stump, I don't know what he meant by that) on the fire to burn all night. Well, we no more had crawled into our sleeping bags than the wind started howling. We spent most of the rest of the night stomping out fires from sparks that blew from the stump. We did every thing we could think of to put that stump out but it was just too big. We eventually almost buried it and we thought it was contained, so we went on our hunt.

We didn't spot the big elk the next morning, so we headed for the main camp. When we got into the main camp later that morning, Ron told us that he had been awake most of the night, because Jake (the dog) had spent most of the night keeping a grizzly on the other side of Venus Creek and out of camp.

Our stay at Half-Cabin was quite an experience for me. I had never been in a hunting camp like this before. Every night before we retired and every morning before we left to hunt we had to hoist all the food way up in the air on a pole between two trees to put it out of reach of bears. About the third night it got colder than sin, freezing all of our fresh fruits and vegetables we had been eating. The only thing that didn't freeze was the beer we had in the creek. I wouldn't have wanted to be anywhere else, it was great!

On the third or fourth day Gordy had to make a meat run to get an elk we had killed out closer to the trailhead. He did so because we didn't have enough pack animals to haul our gear and fresh meat at the same time. On the way out, he ran into some forest service employees who told him that a big storm was forecast and he should get back and get us out or cut enough wood for 7 days so we could stay warm. We got back to camp from hunting about 4 PM and Gordy had also just arrived back in camp. We decided we had to go because the meadow we were in was grazed off and we didn't have a week's feed for the horses. We quickly packed up as much as we could and rode out about 5. Before it got real dark we rode by the spot where we had spiked. To our surprise, although we had buried the stump, it had started a fire that burned an acre or two. Ron didn't know that was where we had spent the first night. He made some kind of disgusted comment about the assholes that had left the fire burning. We agreed with him and never did tell him we were the culprits.

With the overcast skies it was so dark by about 8 P.M. that I couldn't see the white pannier cover on the packhorse right in front of me. I was bringing up the rear and Mark would holler at me every few minutes to make sure I was still there. Gordy was in the lead most of the way. His horse missed a river crossing and the next thing you knew we were all bunched up against a rock wall. Ron was riding a real experienced mountain horse so he let his pony have its head. The horse quickly backtracked a little and found the river crossing. We let Ron lead us out the rest of the way. We rode in the dark, rain, snow, and fog and finally got to the ranger cabin where Gordy had hung the meat. That cabin was about 70 to 80 % of the way back to the trailhead. We started to load it on Gordy's gray mule by flashlight and for whatever reason the mule started bucking, spread his load all over the place, and ran off into the woods. Finally we got him rounded up, calmed down, got everything loaded and headed out. As we approached the trailhead, we could see the glow of campfires of other hunters that were camped there. We hit the trailhead at about 1 in the morning. What a ride! The young horse that I rode almost nonstop since about 8 in the morning must have been one tired pony. Ron made a VCR tape for us covering parts of the hunt and that tape is a treasured memento of mine. Joe's ranch now owns that same horse I rode that day and night. Eleven years after our Greybull River elk hunt, he was part of our deer hunt this past fall (2006). Joe's girlfriend, Karen, rode him our first day out.

In 2002 we went back on the elk-hunting trail. This elk hunt was a late hunt (in December) out of the ranch that our good buddy, Joe, manages southwest of Cody, Wyoming. Joe is another goose camp buddy. We've hunted with Joe out of the ranch several times. It was not a particularly difficult hunt, but this hunt was special because it resulted in the only bull elk I've ever bagged. It was a nice looking 6 x 6 that scored about 320 B&C points. It was not a trophy but any elk that scores above 300 is a keeper to most other hunters and most certainly to me.

My segment of the elk hunt lasted about an hour or so during the first morning of the hunt. We rode out of the ranch down a creek bottom, rode into the first drainage into the creek to our left and then came up the backside of the first ridge to the left of the creek. We walked up a little slope so we could peek over a hump onto a saddle on the ridge. There stood the bull. I got into position, steadied myself, shot and missed…twice. Well geez, the elk had to be 150 yards away. Finally with my 3rd shot I drilled him. He trotted a little way north and slid down a steep chute, back down toward the creek. Getting the elk quartered and out of that chute was by far the hardest part of the hunt.

We've been so fortunate to have Joe as a friend, and we've also been fortunate that he's the manager of the Big Hat ranch. The important thing about that, as least as far as hunting is concerned, is that the ranch adjoins public land behind it. Over the last few years we have been on many horseback deer and elk hunts out of the ranch. For as many hunts as I've been on out there, I'm still among the world's worst horsemen. I'm sure I'm a constant source of amusement among the other guys. But that's okay, because I should be better, I just don't pay attention when I should. The ranch that Joe manages has landscaped grounds that border on or are spectacular. There are four or five guest cabins, one of which we stay in when we hunt out there, that vary in size and ornateness from better than anything I could afford to simply grand. There are three trout ponds on the grounds for guests to catch fish from. The main lodge is just spectacular as well as the grounds. Joe does a fantastic job of taking care of it.

Fishing

When I got out of college, I accepted a job running the clinical laboratory at the hospital in Garrison, North Dakota, probably the fishing capital of the state. At the time my experience as a fisherman pretty much consisted of putting a worm on a hook and catching a bullhead. The education I got in the art of fishing in the next seven years was the equivalent of my second college degree. Not that I became a hard core fisherman, but I was making a lot of my own tackle and had bought good graphite fishing rods. Zebco was no longer king in our household. By the time we left Garrison in 1981, I had become pretty proficient and walleye was becoming a staple of our diet.

I hear of people all the time, that say they just love to eat ling (or burbot or eelpout or whatever you want to call them). They can have them. One night many years ago, my wife and I and another couple, Terry and Kathy, were camped far out in the boonies on the shore of Lake Sakakawea. The ladies had retired for the night. Terry and I decided to do a little night fishing. Besides we had some beer we just had to get rid of. We had thrown some lines in the water and were sitting there talking when we had a bite on one of the lines. Terry grabbed the rod and set the hook and got excited because it was obviously a big fish. He got the fish to shore. It was dark and he grabbed the fish by the back of its head. Well, to make a long story shorter, it was a big ling and when he grabbed it, it wrapped itself around his arm. After the screaming and retching died down, I brought a lantern over to where Terry was, and found a thoroughly beaten up 14-pound ling and a slightly crazed grown man.

Our son, Corey wasn't much over a week old when he went on his first camping/fishing trip. We took him just a couple miles out of town to the bay just barely south and east of town. I don't remember how we did, but that was his start in the outdoors. Today he is a very good fisherman; at least some of my love for the outdoors has rubbed off.

When Jamie was about 6 or 7 and Corey 9 or 10, the whole family went fishing on the river below the tailrace. Now this was the first time Jamie had been fishing on a boat, so we anchored the boat on a good spot and sat there and fished. Jamie's method of fishing was to throw the bait out as far as she could, let it set on the bottom for a few minutes and then reel it in, and she usually had a fish. Now all this was pretty much to the frustration of Corey who considered himself a pretty good fisherman. He would fish harder every time Jamie reeled in another fish. Sometimes being lucky is better than being good. More recently, I'll have to admit that last winter; Jamie was the only person that outfished me. I'm not sure any of that was luck!

Our camping spot out in the boonies was kind of a "Why do you camp there?" spot. The best thing about it was that it was hard to get to by ground so there weren't too many other people trying to get to our spot. The worst thing about it was the 30-foot cliff along one side. When the kids were little we literally tied a tether to them so they wouldn't wander off and drop over the cliff. I bet we used to camp there about three or four times a summer when we lived in Garrison. We continued going up there for two or three years after we moved. Last summer we tried to drive out there to check it out, but the Corp of Engineers has locked gates across the trails so we couldn't get there by vehicle any more. It was a nice private place. The camping area being 30 feet above the water made it private. We would walk down a fairly steep trail to a real nice beach. The fishing was excellent there. We used to build fires on the beach and cook there, fish at night, drink beer there, and if we were alone,,,, I'm not going to tell you what we did when we were alone. One night we were sleeping (not on the beach) at about three in the morning. It was pretty breezy and we were actually sleeping on top of the tent that we had taken down because it was so noisy. I woke up and looked west down the lake and could see lightning and faintly hear thunder. It was the last night of the trip so instead of weathering a storm, we got up, packed up and headed home. We just got home and in the house when the storms hit Garrison. We found out shortly after that that tornadoes and very high winds struck on the side of the lake we had been camped on. Lucked out that time!

One weekend we were at our camping spot and down through the pasture comes a big motor home tooling down the trail, headed our way. The guy pulls his motor home up beside our tents, got out and announced his intention to "camp" beside us. He also marched down to the beach, plopped a bunch of minnows that he had in a minnow trap in the lake and sat up his fishing poles among ours. Of course we "welcomed" him with open arms. We could have shot him we were so irked, but of course we were civil to him. Thousands of miles of shoreline and he comes and parks his motor home by our tents! Early the next morning Rob went down to the beach and cracked open his minnow trap so the minnows would slowly escape. We were down on the beach fishing a little later when the guy came down to fish. He pulled in his trap and it had about 5 minnows left in it. He was mad and came marching over to us and asked us if we had stolen his minnows, to which we honestly replied "No". He grabbed his poles and his trap, stomped up to the top of the hill, got in his motor home and left. None of us ran after him to apologize, in fact, we thought he should have apologized to us. Some people would call what we did vindictive, but we just called it getting even. I know the civilized thing do would have been to grin and bear it, but then just being from way out here in North Dakota, a lot of people already question our civility. I'm sure in his mind he didn't even realize he had done anything to offend us. Anyway, happily, we never saw the guy again. Good riddance

In July of 1980 I fished the ND Governor's Walleye cup with old friend and fishing buddy, Marlan. Now Marlan isn't the most comfortable person in a boat in high winds. Because, as we related earlier, he had a boat sink on him a year or two before that, understandably, he gets a little nervous when the water gets rough. The first day of the tournament it rained, the lightning flew, and the wind blew (hey, I'm a poet) and the second day just the wind blew so as a result we never got to fish a spot that I wanted to because it was too exposed. We did just terrible, I don't think we caught more than a couple walleyes.

I had the Monday following the tournament off, so naturally I went fishing. I went out to Steinke's Bay (about 3 or 4 miles southeast of town), went out to the shallow flats at the mouth of the bay, dropped a line in and immediately caught a walleye. I ended up boating seven with the last one being a 32 1/2-inch fish weighing over 11 pounds. They quit biting as soon as the breeze that was blowing when I got out on the water quit and I lost my walleye chop. A walleye chop is just riffles or waves on the surface of the lake that lower the transmission of light, or to put it simply, keep it darker under the water. As Don Adams (Agent 86, Maxwell Smart) would say "we missed it by that much". On the bright side there are relatively few people who can say they've caught an 11-pound plus walleye and I'm fortunate enough to be one of them. And I also made the Fargo Forum! John Lohman, outdoor editor of the Forum, heard about what I did and put a short article in the paper. A couple years later I was at a fishing seminar in Bismarck where outdoor writer Dan Nelson mentioned it also, which was nice although he embellished it quite a bit. Not that I minded, everyone should be allowed his or her 15 minutes of fame.

One day in the late 70's (we lived in Garrison at the time) fairly early in the morning there was a knock on our door. When I answered I discovered a couple of fairly elderly gentlemen. They said they had talked to a couple guys downtown and had been told by them that I would be a good river fishing guide for them. I explained to them I had never done that before, but since I wasn't working that day I would be happy to go with them and show them a few things. So I grabbed a fishing rod and threw a little tackle in my pockets and we headed to the tailrace. When we arrived, they said they would like to try fishing the chutes (the fast water just below the dam). Now the chutes are not an easy place to fish. The area is lined with rock and unless you keep your jig, or whatever you are fishing with, dancing above the rocks, you will be constantly snagged up. They were constantly snagged up and for some reason I was catching fish one after the other on an old grass green colored standup jig and a minnow. Even other boats around us were hollering over to our boat asking what I was fishing with. The old guys were convinced I was superhuman. At that moment in time I was, for some reason!

Fishing in the chutes on the tailrace can be a real adventure because of the rocks, but also because you never know what you're going to catch. It might be a salmon, steelhead, brown, rainbow or cutthroat trout, northern pike, ling, sturgeon, walleye or sauger. The tailrace is renowned for its big fish of many species, especially trout. A Chinook salmon in excess of 30 pounds has also been caught there, as well as brown and rainbow trout in excess of 20 pounds. So what I'm about to tell you is not all that unusual. Once in the chutes Rob and I were catching walleyes drifting with nightcrawlers on Lindy rigs. I had a bite and this one really took off. I could tell immediately it wasn't a walleye. When it jumped shortly after I hooked it, I could see I had a trout. When we finally landed it we had a beautiful 10-pound rainbow trout. Another time I was by myself in the tailrace's "honey hole", just off the dock. I had caught a couple walleyes when I had a vicious hit. It ran, it jumped, and it fought. When I landed this fish it was a 12+-pound brown trout. I've also caught a 4½-pound cutthroat trout in the "honey hole". Those are really magnificent fish.

During the time we lived in Garrison, I believe the year was 1978, I was able to witness one of the most remarkable things I have ever seen. In the spring of that year, I was down south of Garrison on the lakeshore looking for fishing lures. It had been a snowy, cold winter, so a lot of water was flowing off the plains into the lake that spring. A big ice jam on the Yellowstone River in Montana in the Miles City area had suddenly broke loose and that water was pouring into Lake Sakakawea, also. I was standing there and I noticed the water was rising so fast you could actually see it coming up. The lake level rose 4 feet the day of the lure-hunting trip. The next day it rose another 2½ feet. Six and a half feet in two days! There hasn't been anything like that since. That summer, the flood control tunnels in the Garrison Dam had to be opened wide open. When you stood on top of them, the ground was shaking. They were shoving 66,000 cubic feet per second down the river, compared to a normal 20 to 24,000 cfs. The lake peaked at an elevation of 1854 that summer. That year water went over the spillway, for the first time. That same year, the walleyes of Lake Sakakawea probably had the best spawning season that they have had in the years the lake has existed. It was during the following five or six years that the legend of the lake as a walleye fisherman's paradise was born.

In September of 2002 I was able to go along on a fishing trip into Saskatchewan with a small group of guys from Bismarck. There were 10 of us all together. We drove to a lake named Otter Lake about 40-50 miles north of Lac LaRonge, Saskatchewan. We flew north of Otter Lake for about 45 minutes in a twin engine Otter floatplane. The twin Otter is an amazing plane. We loaded 11 passengers and a huge amount of gear into it and it handled it with ease. Our destination was a lake named Daley Lake. We arrived on Sunday and fished through the next Saturday morning. We caught mostly lake trout and but we also got quite a few northern pike. In our boat we didn't catch any huge fish but we caught large numbers of 6-12 pound lake trout and northerns up to 12 pounds. Those sizes were pretty typical for the other three boats too.

One day we rolled our boat on small logs across a short portage to another small lake where we caught northerns up to eight pounds almost every cast. It was uncanny; I'm sure that all together we caught in the hundreds of pike that afternoon.

But, I've got to tell you it was a very rough trip. We stayed on an island and slept in a couple cabins heated with wood stoves. Oh, did I tell you there was a generator on the island, so we had refrigerators, freezers and regular incandescent lighting? That's right, we also had water heaters and hot showers. I forgot to tell you there was a caretaker who cleaned and gassed the boats for us every day. A Bismarck restaurant owner who is also a very good cook, a little intense, but a good cook, was the leader of our group. He prepared all of our meals, so we did eat well. Except for the cabins, the lights, the refrigerators and freezers, the hot showers, the caretaker and the gourmet meals it was rough, we did have to fish three out of our boat. We could hardly wait to get out of there. When we left the next weekend, I got to fly out in a classic floatplane, an old Dehavilland Beaver. To be honest, in spite of all the 'inconveniences' (or should I say because of them) it was an unforgettable week of fishing.

On that fishing trip one of our roommates was a wonderful man and a good fisherman by the name of Andy. Andy is a great guy whose only apparent flaw was his appetite. He was pretty short and he was almost as wide as he was tall. During that trip we encountered a lot of light precipitation, snow mainly. So rain gear was a must. Andy showed us his rain gear early in the trip. He had bought the biggest pair of rain pants he could find, and had cut off over a foot off each of the legs. I swear to God, it looked like he was wearing a tent suspended on his suspenders. It was comical to see, but they kept him dry.

On one of the days we were fishing we had some extra excitement. My two fishing boat mates, Don and partner Bob, and I had taken our boat into a bay and there ran across a patch of what our fearless leader called 'cabbage'. We had been told and had found it to be true that if you found submerged vegetation you found northern pike. Well we started pitching lures and we were catching northerns almost every cast. We had been there about 15 minutes or so when I caught about a 3 or 4 pound northern that ran directly under the boat. The water was about 5 or 6 feet deep and crystal clear. You could see everything that was down there. Out of the weeds came a huge northern and almost completely engulfed the fish I had caught. But I didn't get a hook into it and after a few seconds it let go of the smaller fish. We have no way of knowing how big it actually was. We tried to get it to bite again, but it wasn't up for a return engagement. That would have gotten me the peaches for sure, but that's another story.

So what's the story about the peaches. Boat mate and business partner Bob brought along a container of canned peaches every day we went fishing. If either of the other two of us in the boat caught a fish bigger fish than a standard we set at the beginning of each day, he would surrender the peaches to the one with the big fish. Well to make a long story short he ate the peaches at the end of every day, which meant that we never beat the size set for that particular day. As I recall we usually had to catch a 12-pound or bigger laker to be eligible for the peaches. We nibbled around the edges but we just couldn't do it. Bob, being the humble person he is, never said a word about it. Yeah, right.

On the way back we drove to Prince Albert and spent the night. We were out to dinner in Prince Albert and were split up over three tables. Our fearless leader let the waitress know that he was the leader and he expected to be served first. When the waitress came to our table to take our order I grabbed her hand and slipped her a $10 bill and winked at her. She took it without hesitation, the other guys at my table didn't even know I'd done it. We were served first and got to listen to our fearless leader moan about it. I never told anyone that the waitress was bribed. Also while we were in the restaurant, before we were served, I stepped out for a little air. There, for the first and only time (so far) in my life, I was propositioned by a prostitute. A tall, thin, fairly pretty native, walked up to me and in a soft voice, asked me if I wanted to party. Of course, I turned her down. She never said another word, she just walked away.

Earlier I told you that if you put a fishing rod in Rob's hand, immediately he would catch the biggest fish, even though he had fished only 10-20% as much as I have fished. This is a perfect example of his abilities. Many years ago Rob and I and our families headed to Ft Stevenson State Park for a weekend of fishing and camping. On Saturday morning Rob and I headed west of the park to what we called Bible

Camp Island. The first drift across a shelf on the east end of the island, Rob immediately caught a walleye that weighed nearly 10 pounds, and then on our second drift he caught one about eight pounds. We caught several more that morning but nothing over three pounds or so, but what a pair of fish! I've never caught more than one eight pound plus fish on any given day. Leave it to Rob. Being the conservation oriented guys we are, since he didn't want to mount the biggest one he caught that morning, we threw it back. He did keep the smaller one though; he wanted his wife and kids to see it, so they could see we weren't just telling fisherman stories.

I think it was the same summer, Rich, my buddy and work mate at the Garrison hospital; was fishing with me in the Governor's Cup tournament. Sometime during the first morning we had found a point that had about a five foot, very sharp break at twenty feet. We caught a couple 2-pound saugers below that break line, but we threw them back. We were looking for bigger fish. Well, the day went all to heck, we hadn't caught a decent walleye and it was almost 3:00 P.M. Our quitting time was 3:30. We decided to run back to that point that had the sauger on it and give it another try. When we hit the point, we figured we had fifteen minutes and then we had to run for home. We netted our sixth and final sauger in about the tenth minute. Those sauger on that point saved our bacon for us that day. We only ended up with around 12-13 pounds but that was much better than 0 pounds. During those years (the 80's), that point was incredible. I don't know if any other guys fished it too, but anytime you wanted to catch saugers, you found that 5 foot ledge on that point and they were always there.

About a year ago, Bob's only daughter and my good friend, Jill married her long time boyfriend, Joe Amsberry, here in Bismarck. Bob thought that a couple days before the wedding it would be fun to go on a short fishing excursion. Joe, Rick (Joe's dad), Bob, our buddy Don, and myself were to make up the fishing crew. Rick had always wanted to fish out here and had brought his boat along with him when he came for the wedding. Rick as well as Joe's mother lives near Park Rapids, Minnesota. The day of the adventure, we got together at Bob's, and decided to split into two groups, Don and I in my boat and the other three in Rick's. We headed north to my favorite haunt, the Garrison tailrace. On the way we picked up bait in Washburn, mostly nightcrawlers, with Don and me picking up a dozen that were dyed green. We got out on the river and downstream from the dam a few miles to my favorite spot. Bob was the first to get his line in the river and immediately caught a small walleye. We fished for a few hours and Don and I limited out using mostly the green worms and the other boat didn't catch another fish. That only goes to prove the old adage that we've all heard at one time or another: "You can lead Bob, Joe, and Rick to water, but you can't make them catch fish!"

More Outdoors

If you knew my brother Rob and had spent any time hunting with him you quickly discovered that one of his passions was chasing fox and coyotes with his pickup. It is, of course, illegal to hunt like that, but as Rob would say "only if you get caught". It was so funny; he was always really torqued at the guys that chased the same animals with snowmobiles. You would have to call that a double standard, I believe. But, you haven't lived until you've been flying down a stubble field at 60 miles an hour while hanging out the window with a shotgun trying to draw a bead on a coyote. One other thing, you very quickly learned that if Rob hit the gas and went down through the ditch, to get your cap off. The button on top of the cap would beat little knots on your head every time you bounced off the ceiling of the pickup cab. And it could and would happen at any time. He had very good eyes.

We also did a fair amount of trapping during the seventies and early eighties. I agree with you that it's not the most humane of sports, but compared to the inhumanity of the ongoing life and death struggles in nature it's actually pretty tame. One morning Mark, Rob and I were checking a set we had placed along a slough. The set was what we called a box trap. It was a rectangular box with one end left open. It had a couple slits cut in the sides by the opening that were there to hold a conibear or what we called a killer trap in position. If anything (we used them for raccoons) tried to enter the box to take the bait that we put inside it would be trapped and immediately killed. When we approached the box we could see something was in the trap. We soon discovered we had trapped a feral cat, and it was still alive,,,and it was pissed. It had somehow gotten into the trap without being killed, probably because it was so slim. We had Rob hold the trap while Mark and I opened the jaws to let the cat out. When the cat got loose it clawed its way up the front of Rob and then up over his head. Meanwhile Rob was flailing away trying to get the cat off him. The cat hit the ground and was gone, Rob was swearing and Mark and I were laughing so that we could hardly stand up. Aah, don't you love the outdoors?

For a few years during our junior high and high school days, Rob and I had a Thanksgiving weekend tradition. What we would do was start up a muskrat trap line on Thanksgiving Day and continue it through Sunday morning. We set up the trap line out on Lake Etta, near Grandpa's place. We would check the traps about every three hours or so and when all was said and done on Sunday, we usually had 150-200 muskrats that we would sell at $1.50 to $2 apiece. That kept us in spending money for awhile. Plus it was a lot of fun. When I went away to college, Rob kept it going with our cousin Darrel. On one of their trap checking forays, Rob broke through the ice in water up to his chest. He and Darrel made a real quick trip back to the farmhouse that day. Rob always liked to go hunting or trapping with Darrel because Aunt Marlene always sent along food. He enjoyed hunting with Darrel and would have gone with him anyway, but the lunch was just an added bonus.

No recollection of outdoor experiences would be complete without mentioning a couple other good friends and companions, Rusty and Tom. Rusty was Mark's golden retriever and was about as good as they get. Tom was my best hunting partner for about 10 years. He was a pointing dog (an English setter) and a true pleasure to hunt over. His official name was Thompson's Ghost, but it was a lot easier to just say Tom. His lineage was that of a champion's champion, he had more field trial champions in his lineage than Carter had Little Liver Pills. A good hunting dog is not easy to come by. You either have to pay big bucks for it or spend a lot of time training it. I chose the latter and as a result also found a new best friend. I'll never forget the day that we went to the kennel to pick out a pup. There was only a few to choose from and when they opened the kennel door, three of the pups came running out to greet us. The fourth took off on his own and went hunting. He was the one we named Tom.

The very first time I took him hunting he was only about six months old. We jumped a covey of partridges just south of Steele. Now instead of running around like a chicken with it's head cut off like you would expect a pup to do, Tom coolly marked the three birds we managed to get. Then, although setters are not known for their retrieving ability, he retrieved all three without a hitch.

One of the ways you train a dog is to give him high praise when he does what you want him to. When Tom was in training, even as a pup, when he found a bird and I praised him, there was always a look on his face that said to me, "I'm hunting, I don't have time for your foolishness". He was a hard working, all business, hunting dog that truly loved to do what he was bred for.

Tom's big problem was with the girls. He was never "trimmed" as they say in the business. We always had the notion that we would use him for breeding. We tried it a couple times, but both times the owner of the other dog failed to recognize what they were getting and were unwilling to pay more than a few bucks for his services. With that great nose he could pick up a bitch in heat from miles away. We had to go into town and search for him several times.

But, he made hunting grouse a pure pleasure and was also a very good dog with pheasants. When we hunted pheasants, because he was such a disciplined dog, you had to constantly urge him on because, as we all know a pheasant will not set still like a grouse. Grouse are just so polite.

When he reached the age of 12 (very old for a large working gun dog) he became terminally ill and we had to put him to sleep. I cried that day at the vet's. I buried him with honors on a very special spot. It was on a high hill, south of Steele, on the exact spot where many years ago we jumped the biggest whitetail buck I'd ever tagged. For the rest of my days he will live on in a very special place in my heart.

CHAPTER 12

MY LIFE REVISITED

I've been blessed with a great life! If you would have asked me when I was young what I thought I would accomplish with my life, I would never have guessed I would have done the things I've done and been the places I've been. I know my life doesn't measure up to that of real world travelers but I'm just a small town farm boy from North Dakota. But I've been to the top of the World Trade Center (while the towers still stood of course) on one coast, to the top of the Space Needle in Seattle on the other coast and stood on the shore of the Gulf of Mexico. I've witnessed the birth of both of my kids and watched them grow up to become intelligent, successful adults. I've been married for 32 years to the prettiest and most wonderful woman I've ever known. I have 7 nieces that I've had the pleasure of watching grow up and witnessed 6 of their graduations from high school so far. I've seen two of them as beautiful brides. Sadly, I've been at the bedsides of two of my siblings when they passed away much too young. I've owned my own successful business along with some fine partners. I've been on what could be considered the ultimate fly-in fishing trip. I've gone waterfowl hunting in the Mecca of waterfowl hunting, Saskatchewan. I've been on several outstanding big game hunts. I've taken what are to me great trophy elk, mule deer and whitetail deer. I've discovered a second 'home' in the

Black Hills that I never knew I had. I've caught many beautiful trophy class fish. I haven't won the lottery yet but I'm working on it. You know what they say; you can't win if you don't play. I've seen my home state from one end to the other and seen a good portion of America. I've created a lot of memories over the years, made a lot of friends, seen a lot of beautiful country and known a fair amount of success, and most important, I've never had the feeling I've cheated myself or for that matter, anyone else. There's still more out there to see and do. I can't think of a better way to spend the rest of my days!

If I had a chance to do anything over in my life, it would be to marry a Dallas Cowboy cheerleader. I'm kidding! I wouldn't change a thing. Even my Parkinson's has served a purpose. It has made me more thoughtful and appreciative. It has also kicked my life into overdrive. Because of it I've done things I may never have done otherwise.

The freedoms I've enjoyed my whole life have been very special, but they've come with a very high price tag. Those freedoms are ours mainly because of our small population and the familiarity that we have with each other. The small population is mostly due to the inability of North Dakota to retain its young people. Of course, there are many other possible reasons as well, but losing our young people alone is a terrible price to pay for our freedoms. That's the downside to living in this far away place. I hope that sometime in the future we find ways to keep more of our young people here. Why? Because I'm a father and no matter how old my kids get, I'll always be a father. I feel we have two special kids and while I'm lucky to have one of them nearby, it would be nice to have the other one at least a little closer so that we can do things together a little more often. In my final assessment of all the things I've done in my life, the things that have meant the most to me are my marriage and the birth of my son and daughter. I can't imagine anything worse than losing a child, either because of estrangement or death.

Over the last few years, I've spent a lot of time thinking about what is **really** important in life, and I think it boils down to these few things. First, if you have children, n**ever, never** pass on a chance to spend time with them, because there isn't anything more valuable than a day spent with your kids. Second, never forget to tell the people you love that you love them every day, or as often as you can. Third, take care of yourself, do things you like to do and don't let your work dominate your life. Fourth, try to live every day as if it is your last and in doing so don't hold anything back or put off until tomorrow what you could have done today. When your life is over, you don't want to have asked yourself too many times, "What if?"